A UNIVERSAL HEART

A UNIVERSAL HEART

The Life and Vision of
Brother Roger of Taizé

KATHRYN SPINK

1817

Harper & Row, Publishers, San Francisco

Cambridge, Hagerstown, New York, Philadelphia, Washington
London, Mexico City, São Paulo, Singapore, Sydney

FIRST EDITION

Library of Congress Cataloging-in-Publication Data

Spink, Kathryn.
    A universal heart.

    Includes index.
    1. Roger, frère, 1915–   . 2. Communauté de Taizé—
Biography. 3. Monks—Biography.   4. Reformed Church—
France—Clergy—Biography. 5. Eglise réformée de
France—Clergy—Biography.   I. Title.
BX9459.S38S67 1987   271'.8 [B]   86-45027
ISBN 0-06-067504-7

87 88 89 90 91 HC 10 9 8 7 6 5 4 3 2 1

To the Taizé Community,

to Dominique Lapierre and to John,

with my gratitude

CONTENTS

PROLOGUE

It was the week after Easter and the tiny French village of Taizé nestling on a hill a few miles north of Cluny was still reverberating with the presence of thousands of young people. Yet in the room occupied by the community's founder, Brother Roger, all was quiet but for the hiss and crackle of logs burning in an open hearth. Perched on a wooden stool, erect and, despite his seventy years, apparently still full of vitality, he confided to me his reluctance, his 'virtual inability' to speak in the first person about his life. 'Why?' he posed the question of himself and answered it after the most fleeting of sighs with another: 'Why me and not the other brothers? I do not wish to crush them with my personality.' ... 'They are all, all reflections of the sanctity of the Church and of Christ in them,' he added. There were other reasons also: 'We never create alone. It is always God who precedes us through the events that occur. God opens the way. It is a human tradition – a church tradition, but not only a church tradition – to seek founders. Yet it is God who founds. Thus the radiance comes from God and not from men. I am embarrassed when people say nice things about us, anything that puts us on a pinnacle. I try to forget them at once. They must be like water off a duck's back. They must not be allowed to penetrate.' The thought apparently spontaneously provoked another: 'You can only build with what you are. It is with our inner wretchedness – that word is a bit strong: it's correct but perhaps it shouldn't be used too much – better say with our inner fragility that God . . . God places his treasure in each one of us in a pot of clay.' There was the faintest intimation of personal sadness, of private struggle, beyond the broad illuminating smile.

In the silence that ensued I took in the honey-coloured glow of the pine planks of the floor and ceiling, and the simple furnishings of Brother Roger's spacious room. In one corner, at the foot of a low bed there stood an icon before which was a prayer mat and a single flickering candle, lost in the afternoon sunlight shining through windows that took up the greater part of two walls. 'Everything in my life appears in colour and light,' Brother Roger reflected, as if discerning my thoughts. 'I remember everything. I don't always remember the exact words used but the substance of the dialogue or a meeting I can recall, and there is always the colouration and the light. Whenever I think of an event in my childhood there is the light and the time of day, whether it was evening, midday or when.' 'When I was young,' he continued, 'my mother encouraged me to spend a great deal of time in the garden because she thought it was good for my health. I have continued to love gardens ever since. When I was in Rome for the Vatican Council I remember looking up at the

Italian sky through some trees. It was as if the trees were actually in the sky. That is what I saw when I was in Rome!'

He invited me to join him at a window overlooking the cluster of village houses and the undulating hills of the Burgundy countryside beyond, and began to describe Taizé as it had been when he had first arrived there in 1940. Yet even as he pointed out the various buildings and their uses, in a scene that must by now be so familiar, it was as if for him the beauty of the landscape still had the power to release fresh inspiration. 'Poetry!' he announced, interrupting his recollections with an air of sudden animation. 'Poetry! – that is what the Church should be,' and he sought eagerly in my expression for confirmation that I had understood and shared in his enthusiasm. He found the wholehearted endorsement he had sought and laughed with childlike contentment. In the aftermath of joy, however, there followed for me the daunting recognition of the impossibility of defining verbally the full meaning and implication of his statement, the reminder of the inadequacy of words and of the hopelessness of attempting to pass on in writing everything that a look or gesture can convey.

We spoke next of intuition, a faculty which Brother Roger saw as a gift from God 'because it allows us to discover God through others'. 'My life', he told me, 'consists of discerning in others that which torments them and that which cheers them and communicating in their suffering and their joy.' In such a life, intuition makes it possible to understand the essential in others, to grasp without many words, to identify another's anguish. 'Intelligence only enables us to understand the surface of another. In the life of the gospel, intuition is there to support compassion, to make compassion possible, to avoid unnecessary dialogue. It enables us to discern the reflection of God. And that is all we can do,' he added. 'We can try to approach the reliefs, the contours of an immeasurable mystery that is God. In our life here we do not know the mystery of God, but we draw near to it a good deal and that is enough for me to live.' Perhaps here too there lay a clue to Brother Roger's reticence. Knowing itself to be poor, Taizé does not profess to hold the answers to this world's problems. It seeks only to be a listening companion to those who seek the one reality, to search with other searchers for the sources of faith, and in this respect as in all others the community and its founder are one.

During the following night Brother Roger, by his own admission, reflected long upon his own reserve: 'We all tend to be reserved in our community life, for fear of burdening others. I hope it is a mark of maturity.' There was a further explanation: 'My father's very noble attitude; that has marked my life. My father was a somewhat reserved man. He did not speak more than he had to, but for that reason when he did speak people listened. Towards the end of his life he said this: "In general in life you do not really know what you have achieved and you might well be surprised to find that what you had thought very valuable to God was not of any great significance and that what you considered a failure had in fact borne fruit." This attitude like so many elements in my childhood marked me greatly.'

That day and on a number of subsequent occasions Brother Roger did speak, perhaps out of a sense of commitment to those who had long been pressing him to do so, perhaps because, aware that past events are sometimes retold in many and varied ways, he preferred to explain himself how things had come about, perhaps because the very act of talking might bring with it new revelations, new dimensions to familiar subject matter, and perhaps too because to speak in some way represented a risk, exposure, and to Brother Roger it is essential to take risks of every kind in life. He talked with his whole body, in sentences that were sometimes incomplete and often modified as soon as they were uttered because nothing must be expressed in terms of absolutes or generalities. Nothing said by him or by his brothers – who also spoke readily of the past and present – must wound, and nothing must close the door to shared understanding. With a combination of the vision that can grow with advancing years and all the spontaneity and wonder more readily associated with youth, he searched visibly for the words and when the words came it was as if it were he who was, to use his own expression, 'most challenged and surprised by them'.

1

A HAPPY CHILDHOOD
IS A HAPPY LIFE

Roger Louis Schutz-Marsauche was born in the small village of Provence, Switzerland, on 12 May 1915. His father,
Charles Schutz, was a Protestant pastor, a man who had
decided at an early age to read theology and who had
pursued his studies first in Berlin and then in Paris and
Switzerland, where for many years he wrote commentaries on the New Testament. 'My father', Brother
Roger recalls, 'was an intellectual, which I am not, but
ever since he was young he had a great love for the poor.
Throughout his life he was marked by – by I don't quite
know what – but what he used to say of his own family life
was that it was Balzacian. My paternal grandfather was
goodness itself. He married very late in life, had just the
one son and took into his home a large part of his in-law's
family.' Nevertheless, Roger's father used to say of this
extended family life and its values that the 'Balzacian life'

meant that he did not have a happy childhood. 'He had', explains Brother Roger, 'a comfortable background, but one that was not free.'

Roger's mother, Amélie Marsauche, was more artistic in her abilities. She came from a French family which had been Protestant since the Reformation. Her grandfather had been a watchmaker whose business had on a number of occasions taken him across the Atlantic in the great sailing ships of the period, a fact which appears to have captured his great grandson's imagination. Amélie Marsauche's grandfather had died at an early age of tuberculosis, leaving two daughters and two sons, of whom the latter were to die of the same illness. Roger never knew the great grandmother who was left a widow while yet so young, but his elder sisters and his mother frequently spoke of her and he admits to sharing with her the habit of reorganizing in imagination the interiors of houses. Perhaps, he deduces, it was the pain of personal loss that induced her to fall asleep while mentally moving furniture. As for him, it is impossible for him to live in a house without, in imagination at least, rearranging its contents.

Amélie Marsauche's family was one in which music had always played a prominent role. One of Roger's great aunts in particular had studied music at Weimar for four years under von Bülow, and her university diploma was subsequently signed by von Bülow and Franz Liszt. The whole family was impressed and influenced by this aunt who was so talented a pianist and who was later to give Roger's sisters music lessons and teach them *solfeggio*, but it was Amélie Marsauche who first seemed likely to follow in her relative's footsteps. She studied singing in Paris where her family lived, thinking that she would devote her life to music. Having completed her studies, however, she was approached in a way that was totally unexpected. One day a letter appeared from a family she hardly knew.

It was from Roger's paternal grandparents and it contained a request for her hand in marriage. 'At the time I could not reply no,' she was to tell her son. 'Such a thing simply didn't exist. So I withdrew to my room. I wept a great deal that day, but that evening I had to say "yes". I was told that I had seen him once at a soirée in Paris. I could hardly remember him and they called that "engagement". It was quite extraordinary!'

The fact that Amélie had so little to say in the matter did not, however, prevent the choice of the marriage partner from being a good one. Despite the fact that their visions of life differed in many respects, Charles and Amélie Schutz complemented each other well. Roger's father was much more rigorous in outlook. He was a man for whom intelligence counted a great deal, who set himself almost impossibly high standards. He was capable of speaking perfect German, for example, because he had studied in Germany but he did not like to do so because, he maintained, 'one should not speak a foreign language to grate on other people's ears'. Roger's mother was more supple by nature, less severe: 'My mother had had a very happy childhood and that found its expression in her constantly. She never scolded. From time to time her elder brother had provoked her father's anger. She could not bear it and would rush to her room. Often she would say, "When I hear someone scolding, losing their temper, to me it's as if they are out of their minds."' Vivacious, yet possessed of apparent serenity herself, she had the capacity to appease her husband's less even temperament.

Amélie Schutz was a dedicated letter-writer. Each morning was devoted to maintaining a correspondence with a wide variety of people, and only recently her letters to one Mother Abbess were used in the beatification of one of the Sisters of Unity. During the earlier years of their marriage Amélie would also spend her evenings copying out the texts of her husband's biblical commentaries. The couple shared a liking for music. Charles Schutz played the violin although not exceptionally well. Above all, however, they shared a love for the poor, a love to which Roger's mother gave ready expression and about which Roger's father said very little but which he experienced nonetheless profoundly. Together they moved to the village in the Swiss Juras where Roger was born at a time when his mother was suffering from tuberculosis. The opportunity to take the mountain air was all that could be recommended at the time. In Amélie's case, however, it proved to be effective. The climate produced the necessary cure and Charles Schutz became deeply attached to the population of very poor people in the mountain village, responding to needs that were instantly apparent. 'When my father arrived, there had just been a murder in the village. A drunken father had killed his wife and children with his gun, then set fire to his house and killed himself. My father arrived after that! In the village people used to make alcohol out of gentian roots and the alcohol they brewed clandestinely in their homes made them utterly ill. The men did not work any more, or very little, and everyone was poor!' In an attempt to alleviate the problem, Roger's father put a stop to the sale of absinthe in the village, but his action provoked a desire for vengeance. One evening a large stone was thrown through the window of the pastor's house and landed on the pillow of the bed where one of Roger's sisters slept. It was only by chance that she happened to be away that night.

Thus it was in what Brother Roger has described as a village 'as poor as possible' that he spent his earliest childhood years. He was his parents' ninth and last child. Another baby born shortly after him failed to survive; his only brother was considerably older and so it is his seven sisters who feature prominently in his early recollections.

It was they who at his birth gathered to choose for him the name of Roger, a name he loves for that reason. 'I was very much influenced in my young years by the fact that, coming after so many girls, I couldn't actually be brought up with them. There was no sense of isolation at all, but the last of the girls, Geneviève, was always at the piano, even when she was very small, so we did not play together. Thus it happened that I played a good deal on my own. I played very readily with other children too of course, but I had only two male cousins who lived too far away to come to me. Solitude in the garden left a very deep impression on me: beauty, the discovery of everything there was in it, a woodpecker, a whole host of things that had their roles to play in the life of the garden.'

A number of incidents recalled reinforce the impression of a somewhat solitary boy in an essentially female environment, in which his mother was too busy coping with the requirements of an extensive household and eventually with an invalid mother to devote very much time to him. Amélie was, reflects Brother Roger, 'serene and joyful and tender by nature with a heart that was maternal and welcoming towards everyone,' but the very warmth and generosity of spirit which brought so many guests to the house must have meant that the demands on her time were manifold. She herself told of how one spring, a year after Roger was born, towards midnight she came to kiss him goodnight in his cradle only to find that he was not there. Her heart missed a beat until it was suggested that he might be in the garden. A search revealed that, sure enough, Roger was asleep under a tree. He had been forgotten in his pram. On another occasion when Roger was slightly older, a friend of the family who had never seen the boy before was surprised to run into him one morning in the garden. Scooping him up into her arms she carried him to his mother exclaiming that she had thought the child was kept hidden because he was abnormal. 'Oh, he will be pleased that you're taking an interest in him,' was his mother's response, 'because I don't have much time for him.' 'And yet,' insists Brother Roger, 'I was struck by what my mother had said, because not for one moment did I feel myself abandoned. My childhood, far from being sad and lonely, was full.'

Childhood memories now almost invariably bring with them an outburst of joy. There were the birthdays when he would rush down to find that a peony in the garden had opened in salute. The fact that he had prepared it on the previous day was no impediment to his delight. There was the great aunt whose arrival was always an occasion for celebration, who used to take him for long walks and recount to him the family history, a thousand stories that would have been the substance for countless novels. His mother warned him she was a gossip, but Roger loved to be in the company of one who fired his imagination with colourful anecdotes and who, he claimed, did much to prepare him to be a writer. There was too the young Italian girl employed to help in the house who acted as a second mother to him, washing him in basins of water so cold, the shock of them lingers with him still. There were also the times when he was 'lucky enough to have a temperature' and was allowed to sleep with his sisters in their communal bedroom, and there were the secrets the children carefully guarded from their parents: the pretty little bitch fox-terrier, who had puppies despite Pastor Schutz's instructions that she should not be allowed to do so. 'We didn't dare say anything about them, so we called one of them Moses because he had to remain hidden. We concealed the pups in a cupboard in the girls' bedroom because father never went there. It was just not done. It was all very complicated because the dogs had to be fed there and of course special toilet arrangements had to be made.' Inevitably the dogs were eventually discovered and were immediately given away.

The house was always full of music. There were usually two and at one stage even three pianos in the family home, although not particularly good ones, and at a very early age Roger developed a special love of Chopin, Bach and indeed music in general. His youngest sister Geneviève remembers him singing in his room in an exceptionally beautiful voice, and he recalls a cherished gramophone and records of Tchaikovsky's compositions. So moved was he by this music that he would take the gramophone and hide himself away where no one could find him. 'I would weep from one end of the record to the other and then I would play it again and cry all over again.' In later life he was to prefer listening to music with others. In the company of the brothers, when the pressures of an ever more congested schedule permit, he listens to music, 'through which the plenitude of God is made more accessible' and frequently he listens 'in colours'.

At the age of six or seven, having discovered a collection of books that had come from his father's family gathering dust in a loft, Roger decided he would make himself a library. He was irresistibly attracted to some beautifully bound copies of the *Encyclopédie Française* and so brought them down from the loft together with a number of other volumes. Seeing what he was up to, his mother pointed out that he was bringing down large quantities of dust from the loft. It was his father's intervention, however, that was to leave the most durable impression on the boy. 'Let him do it,' interceded the pastor, 'A happy childhood is a happy life.' To this may be added Brother Roger's own words: 'Childhood images remain for ever the loom on which events are woven and rewoven.'

Of all the childhood images that have remained with Brother Roger perhaps the most significant is that of the arrival at his parents' house of his maternal grandmother. It was shortly after the First World War and Roger was only three or four at the time but he remembers the air of expectation that preceded the advent of this exceptional woman. 'It was late at night when she arrived in the village where we lived, in a car. She was very tired. No sooner had she embraced us than she fainted. In her luggage there was a red blanket. Enveloped in that blanket, she was taken away and after that first meeting I did not see her again for several days. So my admiration must have been all the more exacerbated by the fact that she was apparently unwell, at the very end of her human resources.' A more complete understanding of his regard for the woman who made so dramatic an entrance into his life must have come some time later. 'How was it that I understood what she stood for? It remains a mystery to me. I think my father talked more readily towards the end of his life about the things that had left their mark on him, and he always expressed his admiration for this other mother. His own mother was a good woman but he used frequently to say he had another mother in his mother-in-law, and he admired her precisely because she loved those who were in difficulty.'

During the First World War Roger's maternal grandmother had lived in the North of France very close to where the fighting was being conducted. Two small bombs had actually fallen on her house: one forming a crater in her garden, the other lodging itself, unexploded, in her late husband's books. Nonetheless, she remained there with a daughter-in-law and grandchild, turning her home into a place of shelter and refuge for old people, pregnant women and children fleeing from the battle zone. When, as the invading armies drew nearer, the French officers finally induced her to leave, she travelled with her refugees in a cattle truck to Paris and from there went on to stay with her daughter-in-law in the Dordogne, for her own three sons were away, fighting in the war. It was then that, faithful to her Protestant origins though she was, she used to attend Mass and even receive Communion in the Catholic church.

In the house where Brother Roger's mother was born, guests had still been shown the secret room where in years gone by the local Protestant pastor used to hide during periods of persecution. Yet, as a result of her own devastating insights into human suffering, Roger's grandmother seems to have been penetrated by a deep and enduring desire that no one should ever again have to go through what she had experienced, and to have been led to seek reconciliation. In Europe, divided Christians were slaughtering one another; let them at least be reconciled in order that another war might be prevented. 'She did not seek to justify her action or talk about it, but I understood that by going to the Catholic church she was effecting an immediate reconciliation within herself. It was as if she knew intuitively that in the Catholic church, the Eucharist was a source of unanimity of the faith. Both my father and my mother understood her admirably, but I do not think her other children were very sensitive to what she did. She appeared somewhat stern, more reserved than my mother who resembled her physically, but that was a sign of the times. Human dignity manifested itself in reserved attitudes.' Of his mother Roger was to write when he was older: 'She transmitted the best of herself. In her I read like an open book the gift of herself and yet without realizing it, totally unconsciously, she traced such very precise frontiers that to get beyond them in order to discover an inner truth was not easy.' Even in the grandmother he admired and loved so dearly he discerned an 'unbelievable capacity to hold herself erect, an inner strength and an adherence to the belief that human dignity was of great importance, which sometimes manifested itself in an outer attitude that was a little distant from others'. To one sensitive enough to perceive what lay beyond her outer attitude the elderly lady was nevertheless to become 'a witness, a symbol of reconciliation because she reconciled within herself the strains of the Protestant and the Catholic faith. She made the most extraordinary gestures without wounding the love of her own in the process.' Those two gestures – taking in the most distressed and achieving reconciliation within oneself – were to have a lifelong effect on Brother Roger. Throughout his childhood years all female intelligence was represented for him by his maternal grandmother, and even now he often pictures in his mind's eye his grandmother and the mother, who by her very life communicated to him the meaning of generosity of heart, by the light of the setting sun seated beneath lofty trees surrounded by open fields, in an attitude of welcome.

In the house Brother Roger occupies at Taizé there is only one piece of furniture originating from his family. When Roger moved to the village in 1940 he had the bed on which his grandmother died put on a goods train and transported to France. 'It was a testimony to what I had experienced as a small child with my grandmother and continued afterwards to try to live. We need images. We need to look at, to see and to attach ourselves to what has made its mark on us, to what has impressed itself on us.'

When Roger was five years old, he spent a Sunday with his sisters in the countryside near Estavayer. Towards the end of the afternoon they entered a Catholic church. 'Everything was bathed in shadows,' recalls Brother Roger, 'except for the light that illumined the Virgin and the reserved sacrament. The image remains with me still.' It lingers together with memories of family walks in the Swiss mountains, in the course of one of which his father broke off from the party to enter a Catholic church alone. 'He remained there praying for a long time and emerged without saying anything. This fact influenced me profoundly. If he went to pray there, it must be because he found there something about which he did not speak but which must be very powerful. My mother used to say, 'My husband is a mystic. He needs to go and pray in churches.' As for Roger, he discerned in his father a love of the Church, and an openness of heart which, by his own account, touched him deeply. Almost inevitably his father's example left its mark upon the boy. During a stay with an uncle in Besançon, Roger found himself rising early, before the remainder of the household, to go to Mass in the church opposite. The need for a certain discretion had impressed itself upon him. Returning to find the family at breakfast, the boy was embarrassed to tell them where he had been, as if he had in some way compromised his uncle.

In the village where he lived Roger was struck by the fact that Christians went on Sundays to pray in two different places: some to a church, others to a hall. They even passed each other in the street on the way to their respective places of worship. Yet his own family admired the sanctity of some who prayed in the other place and in general so much love prevailed in the community. It was an atmosphere of harmony to which the Schutz family actively contributed. Among the activities they shared was the preparation of Christmas presents for the poor people in the village. Early in November Roger would spend his pocket money on buying gifts. Family Christmases were shared with motherless children – as part of a sustained concern for those in the parish who were most in need – and there were occasions on which Brother Roger remembers the Schutz children helping people to move to cheaper accommodation, trundling their belongings through the streets in an old pram and depositing them in rooms in which the simple pine furnishings gleamed from diligent polishing with old rags. When he was very young his special task in his own home was to decorate the meal table with flowers. 'We had our meals at a long table. My family liked to invite friends and there were always large numbers of guests present. When I was four or five I would only join them for one meal a day, but one of my sisters who had a great deal of intuition used to encourage me to fetch flowers for all the meals and arrange them on the table. She helped me a great deal in that respect.' More recently an aunt provided a recollection which with hindsight contains a hint of prophecy: when he was a child Roger used to talk very readily about how he would organize his life when he was an adult. Everything was to take place in a large country house where there would always be lots of people. He had planned a kind of 'harmony' for the day and there would always be a generous and expansive welcome.

Although Roger enjoyed the fact that his home was always full of people, inevitably there were certain aspects of the family life from which he found himself excluded. 'I was the youngest and as is always the case with the youngest I didn't take part in the life, the dialogue, that the eldest shared with our parents. That's how it is in any large family. Each one adapts himself to the situation of his age. I never felt that my situation was unjust or distressing, but perhaps that was why I was much more attentive when I did hear a few words.' Impressions he absorbed became the subject of considerable thought and frequently a source of private concern which was heightened by the fact that it was rarely shared.

His father was a silent man with great generosity and goodness in his heart but also a man upon whom the responsibility for so large a family at times weighed heavily. His wife's relatives reproached him for the size of a family which they felt was too large for their sister to cope with. Roger remembers experiences of relatives on his mother's side correcting his manners and behaviour at table in such a way that, even as a child, he recognized implied criticism of his upbringing. Such judgement on the part of his in-laws' family must, Roger deduced, have troubled his father greatly. Sometimes too, when one of Roger's sisters who looked after the housekeeping brought the pastor the little notebooks in which the housekeeping expenses were recorded each month, Roger's father was obviously tense. 'Fortunately, that sister had the ability to laugh and that made him laugh too, but his preoccupation left its impression on me.'

The news that his parents planned to buy a car he suspected they could ill afford provoked a degree of anxiety he would never have ventured to express. 'What do they think they're doing buying a car? They're going to put themselves in an impossible situation!' Then there was the proposed radio: 'A wireless set such as they were at the time, with a large aerial. What were they doing?' The reserve Brother Roger experiences now in sharing with others the concerns that preoccupy him, a reserve which he acknowledges must sometimes weigh upon his brothers, was already with him as a child. 'Alone, I was preoccupied with all this, and in particular with the few words and reflections I heard from my father. My mother preoccupied me less. She was an optimist and I sensed the trust, the confidence, she had in me, but of what my father said I retained the maximum.'

Communication does not appear at any time to have existed very readily between father and son, but when Roger was thirteen an incident occurred which rendered his father less approachable and modified the pastor's attitudes and behaviour substantially. One day Charles Schutz was fetching a heavy bundle of firewood from among a high pile of wood kept in a loft to supply the enormous stoves that heated the house, and as he came down through a trap door the door slammed shut causing him to fall on his head. Anxiously the family waited at his bedside, expecting the worst. The pastor survived, but he was no longer the same man of strength and control he had previously been. The trauma of the experience was to make him less capable of surmounting difficulties and trials and to mean that Roger, even in much later years, found it impossible to present to his father an opposing viewpoint: 'I never answered him back. Inwardly I seethed, inwardly I suffered. I would have liked to respond, discuss things with him but he wouldn't have wanted it. He would not have been able to bear it.' Nevertheless Brother Roger insists, 'I do not regret the need for submission to my father.' It was to teach him the forbearance he would need in years to come.

To Brother Roger, analysis of the past is suspect. He considers it impossible to discern which people, events or circumstances are really influential. What matters, rather, is that in his encounter with others he should be fully in the present. Nevertheless, in the example of his parents he is prepared to perceive the shaping of his vocation: 'Although we never discussed the matter, my father had great confidence in the study of the sources of faith. He was a man of faith, a man who daily read *The Imitation of Christ*. And so from my very earliest infancy I saw my father who loved the Scriptures, and I saw my mother who loved to write her letters and I think there was, by a kind of osmosis, a need in me to do as they did.'

Family reading was also to exert its influence. 'In France in those days it was customary to read as a family. In my mother's family her father used to read aloud and the practice was passed on. In the afternoons we would assemble to read the works of writers and novelists such as Balzac. I think it was my mother who chose the subject matter. My father did not take part but we read among other things fragments of the history of Port Royal des Champs by Sainte-Beuve. We never read the history in totality but always the same extracts which I think perhaps my father may have discovered in the first instance.'

Port Royal des Champs was originally a Cistercian convent, founded in 1204 in the Vallée de Chevreuse to the south-west of Paris. By the beginning of the seventeenth century it had become more of a boarding school than a monastic community. Under Louis XIV it was customary for influential families to send their unmarried daughters there at a very young age. A dowry was paid to the convent and in an atmosphere of relaxed discipline, the young women dressed in fine clothes, paraded their jewelry and generally led a life which bore little resemblance to a religious vocation. It was customary, however, for the Mother Abbess of the community to be appointed well in advance. Thus in 1602 it was decided that Angélique Arnauld, the daughter of a Parisian jurist should be the next abbess of the community. At the age of seventeen, she was compelled against her wishes to accept the appointment. Having previously shared without protest in the liberal atmosphere of the house, the young abbess fell subject to great inner turmoil. She became ill and it was during a period of personal anguish that she heard a sermon preached one Sunday morning on the theme of grace, that unconditional gift of God. In response to what she saw as God entering the life of the convent, she promptly introduced, with the support of a few who chose to follow her leadership, drastic and far-reaching reforms.

It was this period in the history of Port Royal des Champs and the person of Mother Angélique that earned the admiration of both Charles and Amélie Schutz. Amélie Schutz kept a framed photograph of Angélique

Arnauld, referring to her as her 'invisible friend' and Roger was captivated by her: 'It was not so much the reforms themselves. They were extravagant perhaps. Her reactions were those of a very young girl. She closed the grilles, closed the doors, closed everything. What interested me was what that woman and the women who followed her were; that this girl who did not want the task, who had her office thrust upon her when she was so very young, should have chosen God, chosen to love. I admire the profound choice she made in the most difficult, the most unlikely circumstances, and the fact that a few women in the seventeenth and eighteenth centuries could have such an influence on the course of history . . . not that we at Taizé have ever had any pretentions to changing the course of history and I hope we never shall have.' Somewhere in Brother Roger's studies of Port Royal, there dawned, too, the conviction that an authentic monastic life, imbued with the spirit of renewal, contained within it a unique power to accomplish a special vocation within the Church.

Pascal was the other great name to be associated with that of Port Royal, the birthplace of Jansenism. But if Pascal appeals to Brother Roger it is not the polemical Pascal but the Pascal of the *Pensées*, the spirit of which may be summed up in the words: 'It is the heart which senses God, not reason. This is what faith is: God sensible to the heart.' It is not the puritanism of Jansenism which attracts but the search for freedom and creativity in conformity with what may be discovered from the gospel.

Part of Roger's education was undertaken at home: 'My father made me study. He loved teaching so much. As for my sisters, the eldest ones even had governesses. I think my grandparents must have helped financially at that time.' At thirteen, however, Roger was to embark on his secondary-school education in a town some distance away. It meant living away from home and his parents were careful in the selection of accommodation for him. 'There was a poor woman who had just lost her husband. She was left with numerous children and nothing on which to bring them up. My parents knew that Madame Bioley was a woman of deep Catholic faith, that she took Communion every day, and they chose her because she needed the rent that they would pay. They made a choice that showed great generosity of heart.'

The apartment into which Roger moved was spacious. The furnishings of more prosperous days still remained and the walls were hung with family portraits, yet beyond these vestiges of relative prosperity lay a carefully concealed poverty. 'The family was short of money. I was careful not to tell my parents, but they could hardly stretch to heating the room in which we used to eat. What was not lacking, however, was a profound trust in God. We celebrated the Catholic feast days as a family and their faith touched me to the maximum, to the very highest degree. A few years ago I saw Madame Bioley's eldest daughter again and she reminded me of how I used to talk so much to her mother at mealtimes and went on talking after we had finished eating. It's true that I admired the way that those women transcended the trials of poverty. Her youngest daughter too was just like her mother – with an inner joy. It goes without saying that having lived with them, the Catholic faith at its most generous, its most essential, penetrated me deeply. Frequent Communion touched me greatly but what struck me most was those two courageous women, the mother and the youngest daughter.' The remarkable qualities of mother and daughter were highlighted by the fact that the remainder of the children were perhaps even more stricken by their father's death and by the hardship of their existence but chose to appear outwardly untouched by it. 'I understood

17

their affliction, but what was surprising was to find in the midst of their pain desert flowers.' 'My parents are generous,' Roger had told himself. 'I am grateful to them for they have chosen well.'

It was this confidence in the integrity and faith of his parents and others close to him that was to help Roger through a period of what he insists was not agnosticism but rather of inability to pray, of silence in the presence of God: 'I could not altogether doubt the existence of God. I have never been able to place the existence of God in doubt. What was in doubt was communion – communication. I could not in all honesty pray. As a small child I had prayed but since then I had been unable to. About that inability, I will only say one thing: I put my trust in the faith of my parents and grandparents. The honesty of my father and mother had always been a fundamental value in every respect. I knew they were honest in what they professed. It was just that they had a vision and an intuition that was not given to me. There was an invisible world into which I could not penetrate, which was refused me. But of course,' he adds characteristically, 'nothing can be forced.' The delicacy and tact of understanding implied by this frequently reiterated phrase seems to stem to some extent from the attitude of his mother who talked very readily and entertainingly of many things but for whom religious faith was a very personal matter about which she preferred to say little. 'I was once amongst a group of women who were praying,' she once said. 'My turn came and I was as miserable as stone. I had to force myself to pray. I did everything possible not to find myself in a similar situation again.' When she was sixteen a pastor had asked Roger's mother whether she was saved. Finding the question scandalous, she did not answer him but to herself she said: 'This man does not know that every night I tell myself that this could be my last and that I am therefore prepared each night to go.' 'What counts with God', she was later to insist, 'is the heart.' The poverty of human expression was something which God would understand.

Brother Roger attributes his own striving for sensitivity of approach, his passion for listening to others and his desire for an understanding of that 'great ocean that is the heart' to the darker, even painful, interludes in his life: 'When the storms come, in the darkness where there is so little light, instead of turning in upon ourselves, we may come to realize that it is by this means that a heart open to all is created, engendered in us. We may discover something of the truth about our person, a little of what constitutes it, and from that moment onwards we want to understand others, to be with them, not to give advice – because in that way we risk making vast errors – but to be there to listen to them.' The seed, at least, of this insight was sown while Roger was in his teens, at a time when he fell ill with tuberculosis, possibly in part as a result of his stay with the Bioley family, for the youngest daughter was to die of the disease and, although he was careful to say nothing of his experience to his parents, he recalls witnessing her progressive decline.

Roger was ill for several years, during which there were intervals of apparent improvement and relapse and even a time when he came very close to death. During the first stages of his illness he was nursed at home until it was thought that he was cured. At this point, however, he was taken to Geneva to undergo a series of tests, after which the specialist announced that his condition was worse than had previously been stated. He wanted to send the boy to a cure resort and gave Roger's parents instructions to that effect. Pastor Schutz, however, remained firmly opposed to the idea. A young friend had just died in a similar resort. Consequently Charles Schutz insisted that if his son was going to die it would be better for him to do so at home. So grave was Roger's condition that the doctor would only release him after his parents had signed a paper to the effect that they accepted full responsibility for their action. 'So I was taken home to wait for death. I prepared myself to go with very great serenity as young people often do. What I did find difficult to bear, however, was all the relatives coming to see me, and their anxiety. As by this time all my sisters had married except for Geneviève, the youngest, I asked her to see that they did not come too much. If I had died it would have been in the little bed that used to be my grandmother's.'

Roger's recovery was a slow and protracted process. Eventually the cavities in his lungs calcified but not before he had spent a period of enforced solitude during which he read, studied and eventually managed to take long walks in the mountain air. 'It took years. I never talk about it because it was a period when solitude was intensified by the very nature of the situation. Yet,' he insists, 'that period was beautiful – remains beautiful. They were difficult years but years during which one was very aware that one was building oneself, shaping oneself. A God of love and compassion does not inflict suffering,' he asserts, 'but man can make use of it. It is not only from happiness that creativity stems.' With hindsight Brother Roger recognizes that he has managed to traverse other difficulties more serenely because he came so close to death at an early age. He also realizes that 'the illness contributed greatly to the future, because in it the call of God seemed to be implicit although I couldn't manage to understand it at all'.

At the time Roger looked upon the reading and study that occupied his convalescence as the ideal preparation for a career as a writer. It was a calling that his mother readily understood and encouraged. Charles Schutz, however, was steadfastly opposed to the idea, and his reservations were endorsed by the fact that one of his brothers-in-law who had also been a friend of his youth had failed to make a success out of a literary career. At first he had written works of literary criticism on Ibsen and Bergson and they were reasonably well received but the remainder of his work had been little read. For Roger's father this was flagrant proof of the impossibility of living by the pen, and Roger had to listen to him; the pastor could not have borne it otherwise. Alone Roger did the work necessary to qualify for the faculty of literature. Two of his married sisters attempted to intervene with their father on his behalf but Charles Schutz remained implacable; his son should read theology.

Such an insistence might at first seem strange on the part of a man who had for some time wanted to abandon the ministry and who was ultimately to take early retirement because he found his position within it so intolerable. Had Roger's father remained in Provence he would have been happy to continue his ministry. One Sunday morning in 1927, however, a group of Protestant church leaders for the canton, dressed in black, arrived in the village church of Provence intent upon inducing the pastor to move away from the parish he loved to Oron.

The appeal was made because Charles Schutz's pastorate was so greatly appreciated. He was, it was maintained, needed in Oron, and the pastor found himself unable to refuse this the last of a number of such requests. In 1939, however, the very same men were to put pressure on him to leave Oron because he was not sufficiently 'modernist': 'A very short time after his arrival he was criticized for not being a modernist. For him there was no question of following a trend that marked a particular time. It was known as liberalism, modernism, and meant the rejection of miracles, of the resurrection. It was not my father's vision of the gospel, yet my father was a man of faith.' Twice the church leaders of the canton visited Pastor Schutz in his home. A heated exchange was heard to take place in his study, in the course of which this man of the New Testament was taken to task on the grounds that he propounded a theology that was insufficiently based on the modern sciences. According to Brother Roger's mother, one of them was even reduced to shouting. To her such behaviour was incomprehensible and to her husband such scenes represented the kind of obstacles with which he could no longer cope. The confrontations seem in some way to have broken something in Pastor Schutz. Yet, among scattered references to experiences of this kind, only the most oblique criticism may be inferred on the part of his son of a form of Protestantism which purported to be democratic in that decisions were subject to a vote, but which was so autocratic in its dealings with Pastor Schutz. His inability to surmount such trials accentuated by his accidental fall, Pastor Schutz resolved to leave the ministry, and indeed the country, to run a small farm in France, his wife's country of origin. He was not, however, physically strong and those who were close to him made a concerted effort to dissuade him. Accordingly he confined himself ultimately to taking early retirement in Presinge, near Geneva, an apparently stern but, it seems, a tired man. The trauma of his accident combined with the knowledge that he was no longer wanted made him tense and even more silent than hitherto. His enthusiasm for exegesis and the Scriptures, however, remained unshaken and, as far as his son was concerned, he saw the study of theology as 'a means of opening doors', an undertaking which would give him direction in life and which would not necessarily entail any further commitment.

Brother Roger admits to being torn between the private

dream he harboured of becoming a writer and a farmer and, on the other hand, the wishes of a father about whose welfare he was anxious and whom he had never been able to contradict. There is a certain irony in the fact that his resolution to pursue his literary interests was not entirely uninfluenced by a feeling of sympathy for his father's desire to give up being a pastor. Concerned by what animated the people who made the decisions that so affected his father, Roger recognized that it was possible to delude oneself by professing to hold a democratic position yet allowing one's heart to become as hard as stone. In the life of the Church all responsibility held must pass through a compassionate heart. In the absence of a pastoral heart filled with humanity, mercy and compassion, such responsibility should be renounced. Such was his reaction at the time and doubtless the experience was to modify his future vision of the Church and of the nature of authority.

Roger's sympathy for and understanding of the pastor's feelings was something which he would have liked to communicate to his father, but which he failed to do. 'I would see him reading, approach him with the intention of saying something but never actually do so.' At the age of twenty Roger set off to Paris to stay with an aunt who had for many years stimulated his vision of being a writer, without telling his father the real reason for the visit. He went armed with an essay entitled 'Evolution of a Puritan Boyhood' which he had written during his long months of illness and of which he says simply: 'One can only write what one possesses within oneself. It was the climax of all the discoveries of my early youth.' How it came about he no longer remembers, but he was to take the essay to the *Nouvelle Revue Française* for it to be read by André Gide with a view to its possible publication. On his arrival, Roger was once more told that he was to meet the well-known writer and critic, Gide. Instead, however, he was introduced to

Jean Paulhan, the editor of the influential review and a critic and essayist of considerable standing, although one less well known to Roger. 'I was with him for a long time and he was very generous, very attentive. He told me he would read the manuscript.' A few weeks later in that same summer Roger received a response with the returned manuscript offering to publish it provided he rewrote the ending. 'I walked a great deal, reflected a great deal, and finally I said to myself, I do not see how I can rewrite the ending. I will not change anything. I cannot. I shall write to Monsieur Paulhan and decline.' Conscience would not permit him to alter something which was so much the product of his personal experience, yet Brother Roger acknowledges that if the advice had come from Monsieur Gide his reaction might have been different: 'Monsieur André Gide was very well known at the time. He was talked about as another Victor Hugo, whereas I did not know Jean Paulhan was a man of letters until much later. So I renounced having my manuscript published and told myself that God had marked that day.' Interpreting this experience as an indication that his literary career was not to be, Roger bowed at last to his father's wishes and applied to study theology for four years at the universities of Lausanne and Strasbourg.

At university Roger felt himself ill-equipped for the course on which he had embarked: 'I was transported into an unknown world, a world of which I grasped nothing and one which I had not chosen. In fact someone there remarked to me one day that I was like a man who had come to a concert and could not understand the music. And it was true.' There was, however, one part of this unfamiliar world which Brother Roger recalls with appreciation. At Strasbourg there was a theologian and historian who specialized in the pre-Reformation Luther. Roger was captivated by what this professor imparted to him of the Luther who questioned. The separations and divisions which ensued did not interest the young man in the same way, but he would go to the professor's room after lectures to continue talking about the Luther that preceded the separation, about his anguish, his unease, his quest for Christian liberty, and he would read avidly about him, evidently captivated by something. Theology itself, however, did not interest him.

In the summer of 1937 the doubts with regard to the wisdom of his choice returned. These feelings were brought to a head when a married sister, Lily, to whom Roger had been very close, fell ill. It was she who had written down the first poems he had composed as an infant too young to write himself, and when she returned to the family home apparently on the brink of death, he sought once more in desperation to pray. 'We were waiting for the end and the only prayer I could bring myself to utter was the words of the psalm: "When thou saidst, Seek ye my face; my heart said unto thee, thy face, Lord, will I seek" (Psalm 27.8). These words seemed to me honest. My heart called upon me to say them to the living God.' Roger's sister recovered, and for her brother her recovery was a divine response. He felt himself impelled to continue along the path on which he had embarked. 'Afterwards certainty came when I was reading an old edition of a sixteenth-century book in which I found the direction: It is Christ who enables us to know God. Do not seek elsewhere. An understanding of Christ will allow you to understand God, to have that minimum of understanding of God. That was a very powerful point. It brought home to me that it was through Christ that those around me looked at, penetrated the invisible, perceived a reflection of the unseen.' To those who now find the person of Christ more of an obstacle than an aid to belief in the great mystery of God he offers a suggestion rather than a directive, undoubtedly based on his own early experience: 'I would perhaps say, "Remain attentive to those who see things differently from you. They are often honest and they perceive in Christ something of the invisible that he has been manifesting to people across the centuries. Do not close yourself. Live the little bit of gospel you have grasped." ' To Brother Roger, God, like the human heart, is to a large extent indecipherable, inexplicable. To profess to understand the whole is thus not necessarily a good thing. Rather what is important is that man should constantly try to approach the reliefs and contours of a mystery beyond our comprehension. The search, whatever form it takes, is of significance, but in that search Christ can help us to fathom much, and the Church – the mystical body of Christ – remains an ever present source of comfort and companionship. Why worry then that we do not fully comprehend the mystery of God, for the totality of the Church may understand?

Another event of decisive importance for Brother Roger's future life was to occur during his final year of university studies. 'It was 1939. The war was beginning. I was returning from Strasbourg to Lausanne. I got off the train to be met by someone who said to me: "You must accept the presidency of the Christian Student Association".' Roger had already received a letter inviting him to assume the position and had declined to do so. 'I had only been to one of their meetings and that I had not liked. I had withdrawn immediately and never went a second time. There was simply no question of my being their representative. Besides what were they thinking of in choosing me. I was not at ease myself. Couldn't they see that?' Nevertheless, touched by the persuasion of those who had elected him, Roger found himself assuming the role for which he considered himself so ill-suited. It was a step which he now sees as a constructive one, because it

26

brought him into obligatory contact with other young people. 'From the very beginning it was a question of seeking the sources – although at that time we referred to them as the "foundations" – of faith, of not only looking at the Scriptures but of questioning ourselves on religious faith.' During that period the question of 'science and faith' was a prominent issue. Meetings were held in the faculty of literature at Lausanne, first in a dining hall, then in an amphitheatre and later, when even more room was needed, in a large auditorium in the university. Young people, it seemed, were as eager then as they are now to search.

Out of a group of regular attendants of these meetings a year later, under Roger's leadership, the 'Grande Communauté' was to be born. This was a kind of 'third order' which would meet regularly for colloquia and for the retreats, which Brother Roger has described as 'necessary for much converse with God and little with his creatures'. The retreats attracted a substantial number of people. However, popular as they were, by the summer of 1940, when Roger needed only to complete a short thesis to finish his studies, the gatherings of the Grande Communauté had become but a part of a much larger perspective.

The solitude, the long walks, the reading and the contemplation undertaken between the ages of seventeen and twenty-one were to bear fruit. During his walks he used to go into an isolated little parish church and there he would meditate upon the idea of a community. During those walks too he would sometimes experience what he refers to as 'a kind of instinct . . . a certainty that something was going to happen'. The confirmation of this instinct was to come during a retreat in a Carthusian monastery in La Valsainte, where Roger found himself captivated by the life of prayer, and by the fact that the monks prayed and lived in community. So great was his interest, that his father was afraid that he would never leave. The strictly contemplative and restricted community life of the Carthusians was not, however, for him. 'It was not a question of living as they did. They each lived in their house with a community life that was confined to a meal together, once a day or perhaps only once a week, and a walk together once a week. From my cell I watched them coming and going in the snow ... but it was their life of prayer that gripped me.' To one who had experienced anguish because of his apparent inability to communicate with God, one aspect of spiritual life in community emerged as particularly attractive: 'someone else praying because one prays very little, very badly oneself'. Initially, however, despite the attractions of community, Brother Roger recognized that the initiative must be taken alone.

War had broken out. All Roger's family on his mother's side were French and were therefore caught up in the conflict. His brothers and sisters were there too, and so the defeat of France awoke in him powerful emotions. That winter he spent several days in the Upper Juras walking alone, trying to make a decision as to whether he should go to a country which seemed to him to offer broader horizons than Switzerland, where everything he undertook would remain within confined limits. The manner in which he might live in France was also the source of prolonged preoccupation. 'I found myself as if impelled to do everything I could to build a community life in which reconciliation would be realized, made concrete, day by day. To begin with I must start a life of prayer alone. I would find a house where there would be prayer in the morning, at midday and in the evening and I would take in those who were fleeing, those in hiding.' It was thus with a vision of reconciliation not so very far removed from that of his grandmother before him that Roger determined to create a house of refuge and of prayer.

At a time when Europe was torn asunder and some Christians prayed apparently oblivious to the suffering of others, Roger had asked himself incessantly why such opposition and conflict should exist between men and why between Christians in particular. He had asked himself too whether a way existed on this earth for one man totally to understand another and – on a day he remembers well, in a place he could still describe – as the shadows fell one evening he resolved that if such a way existed, a way that meant seeking to understand everything about another rather than to be understood, he must commit himself to it and pursue it until death.

2

A HUMAN DESERT

The surrender of France in 1940 had left the country divided into a zone occupied by the invading German armies and an unoccupied area still controlled by Petain and the Vichy government. Not only had the invasion caused dreadful destruction, but Jews and other political refugees were reduced to fleeing from Nazi persecution to 'free' France and from there to the safety of neutral Switzerland. It was these afflicted people, often stripped of all possessions and starving, whom Roger felt himself impelled to help. In their midst he must live and pray in order that his intuition might become a reality. Accordingly he inquired immediately of a Franco–Swiss agency with an office in Geneva, whether there were any suitable houses available for rent in France. His enthusiasm for the undertaking was not, however, shared by all those around him. At Lausanne Roger assembled his closest student friends:

'I invited those from the science and arts faculties, but no theologians because I told myself theologians would want to chat about God – and only the men, because Taizé was already somewhere in the background.' He told them of his proposed project but the news was greeted with nothing but consternation and disagreement. In the course of a somewhat heated encounter it was made clearly apparent that, almost without exception, the students did not want him to go to France. 'That meeting was a little animated but it did not make any more of an impression on me than it should. I think it was illness that taught me to traverse events that were much more complex than that. They couldn't understand, but we would find each other again.' As a gesture of appeasement Roger promised them that he would return every month or every two months for a long-weekend gathering. By this means he would be able to keep in touch with the 'Grande Communauté'.

Roger encountered difficulty within the family also. He was at home one Saturday when he received a letter from the agency to which he had applied, providing him with the Swiss address of the owner of a house available in France. He resolved to visit the woman in question on the following Monday, but in the interim a misunderstanding occurred about which Brother Roger is reluctant to speak but which was to mark his entire life and which would hasten his departure. Rather than allow this misunderstanding to take hold, Roger felt that it was better inwardly 'to consent to the incomprehensible' and to proceed without delay. So it was that he decided to leave not on the following Monday but at once. That Sunday afternoon he visited the Swiss home of the owner of the property available for rent in France. The elderly woman in question was not at home but Roger waited patiently for her return that evening. He then discovered that the property she wished to let or sell was situated in a valley between Culoz and Ambérieux, only a few metres away from the Paris–Lyon, Lyon–Geneva railway line and not far from a busy road. Roger's instant reaction was that there could be no question of even viewing a two-hectare site in so noisy and busy a location. 'I declined the offer and got up to leave, but then she asked me what I was planning to do and so I sat down again and we spent the evening talking. That woman urged me to go and at least look at the place, and I agreed to go on my bicycle but I was resolute that I would also search elsewhere. Then, at the end of our conversation, she said a strange and beautiful thing. "If you find something else," she told me, "I could give you a loan." A gift I could never have accepted, but I am sure that because it was a loan I agreed at once. We fixed a rate of interest there and then – the normal rate of 4 per cent. It was as quick as that. Of course I did not know how much would be needed, but the knowledge that I could borrow whatever might be necessary gave me an unexpected freedom.' To this day Brother Roger still recalls that when subsequently he bought the house at Taizé for 13,000 francs, the interest was approximately 50 francs a month. On the evening of that memorable meeting, when Roger arrived home late at night he did something he would normally never have dreamt of doing; he banged on the door of his parents' room to tell them what had happened.

Two days later, with remarkable rapidity Roger obtained a visa from the consulate in Geneva. The bridges were down, most means of communication were severed and the trains were not operating, so it was on his bicycle that he set off for Burgundy, ostensibly to visit one of his mother's brothers who was stationed as military chaplain at Bourg en Bresse not far from either Geneva or Macon. Roger did visit the property sited between the railway line and the road as he had promised, but only to have his initial reservations confirmed.

Not far from the Swiss border Roger was to discover a more promising prospect, a property some distance from the nearest village, which had a fine old manor house and a large farm. The woman who lived there was delighted to show him round the house, which incorporated a chapel where St Francis of Sales had once celebrated Mass. She was old and sick and anxious to move into a house in the village next to the church from where she would be able to hear Mass even when she was too infirm to go. She was also willing to let Roger have the estate in exchange for monthly rent until her death. 'She wanted only the minimum, the equivalent of 100 Swiss francs a month which was nothing, because the estate was beautiful, but very quickly I said to myself, "No, it's out of the question. It's too near to Geneva. I would be there all the time. That is not how things are created."' Afraid that he would spend too much time with his parents, now resident in Geneva, if he were to take an estate so conveniently located, Roger left immediately, before he could become too attached to the place. In the following year he was to receive a letter via the woman's solicitor at Saint Julien telling him that the estate was still available to him on the same terms. Knowing the use to which Roger planned to put the house, she was still eager for him to have it.

Another excellent possibility presented itself to him in the neighbourhood of Bourg en Bresse, but once again Roger rejected it on the grounds that life there would be too comfortable to be conducive to creativity. It was a large house set in the lee of a hill with a magnificent view; there were chickens round the door and polished brasses in the kitchen. This was, as Brother Roger put it, 'a land of ease which would lull me to sleep'. After several days of searching, scouring the countryside on his bicycle, Roger arrived at Macon and, having read the history of the nearby monastery of Cluny, determined to visit the site.

Originally founded in 909, the monastery had from an early stage maintained a high standard of monastic observance which was to lead to the adoption of its customs by other houses, old and new. During the eleventh and twelfth centuries in particular, Cluny exercised great influence on the life of the Church and largely inspired the reforms associated with Gregory VII. Its influence declined, however, in the later Middle Ages and the monastery finally closed its doors in 1790. What Roger expected to find at Cluny in the summer of 1940 was an open clearing scattered with monastic ruins. It was not so much that he was attracted by ruins but rather by the association of Cluny with renewal within the Church. 'At that time I had yet to write my thesis on pre-monasticism so I wanted to see Cluny. I slept at La Roche Vineuse, then very early in the morning I got on my bicycle and cycled to Cluny and there it was – a town, and not the ruins I had expected. I went into a shop and asked the shopkeeper whether there was a lawyer and, of course, there were lawyers in Cluny!' One of these lawyers, a Mâitre Bourgeon, was to inform the visitor to Cluny that there were two houses for sale in the area: one in Chateau de Mont, the other in Taizé. Since Roger went first to Chateau de Mont, it was late in the morning of 20 August by the time he reached a rough track leading to a half-demolished and abandoned hamlet situated between Cluny and Citeaux, two poles of monastic tradition. 'I realized at once that Taizé was a poor place. There was no tar on the roads in the area. The road which led into the village was bare rock and the village had been partially deserted since the crisis of the grape crop more than a century previously.'

The house Roger was to view had itself stood empty for several years. The owners, a family by the name of de

Brie, were living in poverty-stricken circumstances in Lyon. It was an old peasant woman from a neighbouring house who showed the prospective purchaser round the property. 'Everything was in good condition,' recalls Brother Roger. 'We have never had to do anything to the façades and the roofs, for everything had been very well maintained. Disaster had struck the people who used to live in the house but they had loved the place.' Most of the land, the former large and valuable vineyards, had already been sold but all the buildings remained: the granaries, the cellars, the wine storehouses, the press, sheep pens and cattle sheds – and to the visitor's amazement they were all for sale for the price of two cars, one for the buildings and one for the land. Hungry after his exertions, Roger asked the old woman where he could find something to eat. She explained to him that there were no restaurants in the area but invited him instead to join her for a meal. Together with her daughter she made the stranger welcome. During the meal Roger talked to them and when they had finished eating the old woman made a poignant appeal: 'Stay here, we are so alone. There is no one left in the village and the winters are so long and cold.' The words of a poor and ageing woman were to prove decisive. The Christ who in St Matthew's Gospel identified himself so specifically with the poor, the hungry, the thirsty and the lonely, had spoken.

Returning to Switzerland, Roger recounted his experiences to his parents. He did not mention the property with the oratory in which St Francis of Sales had celebrated Mass, which he could have had for a small rent. His reluctance to spend too much time with his parents in Geneva would have hurt the father he was constantly afraid of distressing. He did, however, speak of his exchange with the woman at Taizé. 'Did anyone say anything of the kind elsewhere?' inquired the pastor.

Discovering that it was only at Taizé that his son had received such an appeal, Charles Schutz's pronouncement was unwavering: 'God speaks through the poorest of the poor. You must listen to the humility of that humble woman.'

In Roger's eyes the fact that Taizé was sited within two kilometres of the demarcation line and so very close to the suffering of the moment represented an additional attraction. It was also to become symbolic of his later life, a life spent on the demarcation lines that divide humanity. So it was that, by no means oblivious to practical considerations, in September Roger went back a second time to look at some of the properties he had already visited. This time he was accompanied by his brother who, as a farmer, was more familiar with agricultural matters. In his brother's view the house and land close to the Swiss frontier would be the best value for money and hence the wisest choice. Taizé, he informed Roger before leaving, was worth nothing. Despite such objections Roger returned to the lawyer's office in Cluny to sign the promise of sale. Considering him to be very young to be signing such an undertaking, the lawyer pointed out to him that once he had put his name to the paper he would still have to pay a quarter of the sum involved, even if he should change his mind. Telling him he would return later, Roger went to the church of Our Lady in Cluny to pray and gather his thoughts.

Roger signed the undertaking to purchase the property and the lawyer promptly sent a telegram to Lyon to the owners of the house. What the purchaser did not know then, but it is a story that has since been well substantiated, was that the very day on which she received the news that the property had been sold was the ninth day of a novena Madame de Brie had been offering that their house might find a buyer. 'The lady who owned the house was a fervent Catholic,' one of the Taizé brothers remembers, 'but her husband apparently was more a follower of Voltaire than of Christianity, as people were at the time in regions like this, areas which some consider had been de-Christianized since the French Revolution and which others believe had never been strongly Christian. The churches were deconsecrated and there were no more priests. Still, that woman had offered a novena which finished on 8 September, and on her return from Mass that very day she received the telegram. She and her husband had nothing left to live on. They had one child, a boy who bore the Christian name of Roger. We invited them to come and stay here, and it was through her that we learnt all about the history of this area. She was a woman of exceptional ability.'

In the years that followed, Mme de Brie was to become a frequent visitor to Taizé where she was known affectionately as Tante Mathilde, and in her later life she was to remember a letter she had received in 1923 from a Benedictine nun at Dourgne with whom she had shared a spiritual correspondence. Sister Hildegarde M. Loicat OSB had never been to Taizé but, in her letter written seventeen years before Brother Roger's arrival in the village and dated 25 January, she describes a dream which has a certain relevance to the community that was to be born there:

I cannot resist the thought that came to me in the choir that I should recount my dream to you. It is only a dream but so lovely.

At the moment we are reading the religious history of France by George Goyau. In the last few days we have been in the golden age of Cluny and naturally I have been thinking of you who live on Clunian ground.

Last night I was transported to Taizé (which I know from a card my sister Thilde sent me a short time ago).

There I found monks singing the divine office. My soul was overwhelmed with joy. When I asked the name of the Father Abbot, a young man whose blond crown, blue eyes and slight and slender build reminded me of 'our Roger' of whom I have a picture here at the age of twelve, I was told: 'Pierre de Brie'. I wanted to meet him but even as I stepped forward, alas the dream came to an end. What a pity! On waking I completed it.

Perhaps it may be that in the more or less distant future one of your great grandchildren will renew the chain of the past and begin Cluny again. Who knows [inquires the sister] what God intends?

Madame de Brie died in 1977 and was buried in the graveyard of the old Romanesque church in the village of Taizé close to the house she had once owned. Brother Roger himself did not attach undue importance to the dream. However, some time after Madame de Brie had first showed him the letter, finding himself in the vicinity of the Benedictine convent at Dourgne, he went to see the Mother Abbess and showed her a copy of the account. Sister Hildegarde was by that time dead, but she had been a mathematics teacher and the Mother Abbess remembered her as a 'woman who knew what she was talking about.' The Abbess's reaction would appear to have contributed to the tempering of Brother Roger's initial reservations: 'It was a dream but even so what she wrote has a certain value.'

The choice of Taizé remains for him something of a mystery. Yet in selecting a poor and semi-ruined village he was alone, he explains, and in the silence of the deserts the voice of God resounded. Man in his solitude is sensible to a presence within him and to the mystery of God at work. There are other signposts also to an awareness of a higher purpose: 'When one reads Sister Hildegarde's letter one is made aware that God had foreseen, prepared, opened ways through the thousand events that went before.' Conscious that there are those for whom too easy talk of God, too ready reference to Christ or to the Holy Spirit is suspect, Brother Roger is cautious of the unduly easy use of such language (although it is, he confesses the language of his ethology). Nevertheless, for him God is discernible beyond words, in the simple events of existence.

'I knew', remembers Brother Roger, 'that this project which could not come from me was to take place in a desert. And a succession of events – disease that had struck the vines, the attractions of industry elsewhere, the First World War from which so few of the menfolk had returned – had turned this region, a region of stony ground, into a human desert. As the old woman had said, the winters were long without electricity and solitude weighed heavily, particularly on the elderly, but I don't think I was too afflicted by it. There were too many immediate needs to be met. From the very first day here I had to work, I had to learn how to work the land and live on very little.' The newcomer to Taizé used to make soup out of nettles and eat snails, which he found in profusion because the surrounding woodlands had once been the location for a snailery. 'I used to go and collect them then throw them into boiling water, because nobody here really knew how to cook them, then take them out and eat them just as they were.' Such culinary activities stupified many of the villagers, to the extent that they still talk about them to the brothers to this day.

Nor was it a question of merely providing food for himself. The house, only a few miles south of the demarcation line, was to become the resort of a steady if small flow of refugees, half dead with fear and exhaustion. Brother Roger never asked them for their surnames. They gave only their first names and whatever other information they wished to disclose. He did not want to embarrass them and there was certainly no question of declaring their presence or producing ration cards for them. So the necessity of earning a living and providing a welcome imposed itself from the beginning. With that need, however, came the discovery that it is possible to receive people and to share with very little. Poverty of means, asserts Brother Roger, gives birth to a sense of the universal and to communion, whereas there are times when abundance can be a source of inhibition or embarrassment both to the host and to the guest.

The meals at Taizé have remained simple but wholesome. These days, for example, the supper which guests are invited each day to share with the brothers after the evening prayers consists of a soup to which more or less water can be added according to the numbers present, bread and butter and a piece of fruit. At other times it has consisted only of a cup of chocolate and some dry cakes. What is important is that people can be invited freely. A watchful eye is kept upon the health of the brothers, a consideration which assumes particular weight in fraternities where they frequently share the life-style of the very poor. Furthermore, simplicity is not to be confused with austerity. With imagination, a candle, a flower, the simple things, the little you have, can be used to bring gaiety and a sense of festival to daily existence. This fact and the importance of practical labour as the means to inner equilibrium and communion impressed itself upon him most poignantly during those wartime years when even the most basic necessities of life were in short supply.

Brother Roger has retained warm memories of the welcome afforded him by the villagers at Taizé, and in particular of the elderly neighbour who used to warm a brick in her fire for him to put in his bed at night, and of another 'woman of the gospel' by the name of Marie Auboeuf. It was she who drew his attention to the waxing and the waning of the moon, to the times to plant and sow the beans and other crops, and who invited him to share the warmth of her kitchen stove. 'When I arrived here she was already very elderly, with a face that expressed a great serenity! She and her husband lived in the small house next door. There was a kitchen in which everyone lived, one room for the parents and for the daughters, and the remainder of the ten children used to sleep in the stables.'

Marie Auboeuf had come originally from another village and was a Catholic of very profound faith, but her husband was what was known as a 'free thinker'. It was he who was responsible for the burial of those not buried by the Church, and he prevented his wife from setting foot inside the disused church in Taizé. Mme Auboeuf was known to have a difficult marriage, but in the village she was almost venerated. She took the young newcomer under her wing and told him of life in the village, of how people could only pay for their daily needs after the grape harvest and so existed in a permanent state of debt, and of how they ate maize, vegetables and bread, and meat only on village feast days. She also recounted to him an experience which seems to have enabled her to survive the poverty and hardships of her own existence: 'She never actually said to me, "My husband prevents me from praying," but I knew it was so. One day, however, she told how she was very sick at a time when all the ten children were still small. She was suffering from a form of progressive paralysis and did not know what would become of her young children. One night as she lay in the same bed as her husband in the kitchen, she prayed the rosary – almost certainly, I would imagine, without any rosary beads or any obvious sign because of her husband's violent attitude. There was no electricity at the time, and in the total darkness, she told me, the Virgin came to her.

Afterwards, when she tried to get up, the pains had disappeared and she could walk again. So she was able to raise and care for her children. Obviously she could say nothing about her experience to her husband, but to me, when I first came here, that woman had the face of a mother of the gospel.' It was to her Brother Roger could confide what he was going through, to her he could tell his fears, and she was very quick to understand. In moments of trial, he suggests, there is often solace and vision to be found in people who are nearing the twilight of their lives. He speaks with special tenderness of the 'old peasant women, dressed all in black, their faces lined with the rigours of their existence, the kind you find still working in the fields in countries such as Italy, for they have often given so much and received so little recognition.' Theirs is the fidelity of the women in the Bible who waited in silent empathy at the foot of the cross.

There were many others in a village populated primarily by old people who showed him kindness, and there were others, to whom Brother Roger makes no reference, who made him less welcome. It was his youngest sister Geneviève, who sometimes came to stay in what was at that time called the House of Cluny, who explained that strangers were not always welcome in a village where most resident families had lived for generations, and that Protestants were even less welcome in a community which, although now predominantly de-Christianized, belonged to a tradition of Roman Catholicism. In December 1940 the Grande Communauté held its first meeting in the House of Cluny; it was a relatively short gathering. When the participants had left, it was the concerns of the stricken refugees that were uppermost in Roger's mind. From the very beginnings of Taizé, human beings, victims of the powerful, had been daily present to him in a way that could not fail to evoke compassion.

'When I first arrived, many of the buildings now used for living in were barns and outhouses. The original house had eight rooms and from the entrance which had a huge metal gate it appeared rather small. I had made contact with someone who knew the whereabouts of some of the political refugees, and there was no shortage of people to be hidden and protected. There was a bell at the door and a lock, and I gave directions that I was to be the only person ever to open it. Everyone else was to vanish and hide, and of course there were agreed ways of making oneself known.' For a while the arrangement seems to have worked without major mishap. Roger provided for his guests by cultivating the adjoining land and milking the only cow, and three times a day he would retire to a tiny oratory he had created in which to pray. Many of the refugees were Jews. For Roger there could be no question of making the residents of the house feel obliged to join him. 'It would have been unbearable if they had prayed out of gratitude. What was needed was spiritual tact. They saw me go to pray. The door to the oratory would be open and they would see what was inside, but I would say nothing. You must not force anything. When you are living in the same house you cannot help but bear witness. The gospel teaches us to show the way, to point like John the Baptist beyond ourselves to the way of Christ. But you cannot capture the conscience of a man no matter how beautiful the cause.'

Looking back upon those earliest days Brother Roger views them as years when he was not exactly naive but as a time when he was 'yet without experience of all that constitutes humanity'. It was a time when he was to discover what was least generous, what gave least cause for joy about humanity, and a time when he was in constant danger. For the first two years Roger's parents had asked General Filloneau, who was an uncle through marriage of one of Roger's sisters, to keep an eye on their son from a distance. In May 1942, however, Roger received a letter from the General saying that he could no longer protect him. Too much had been noted against him. General Filloneau advised Roger to leave Taizé but the young man chose to remain, despite regular visits from the French civil police who were determined to ascertain what was going on in the house. He remembers telling himself to 'consent' to whatever might be in store for him, be it deportation or death, just as when he was in his teens he had resolved to consent to his illness and possible death. 'It was hot, the windows were wide open. I was sitting down writing. In the face of the fear that gripped my innermost being there was yet a "yes" to God. I consented to his will for me and offered him this prayer: "Take my life if you see fit, but let what has begun to mature in this place continue."'

In November 1942 Roger helped an escapee from the Nazis over the French border into Switzerland. In Geneva he gathered money for his work with the refugees and was on the point of returning to Taizé when Gaston Chautard, a friend in Cluny, sent word advising him not to return. On 11 November, as soon as the Germans had entered the hitherto unoccupied zone, the Gestapo had twice visited the house in Taizé. 'I discovered that the so-called free zone was not free at all. Someone had been interrogated and had denounced me and what I had been doing. It was in 1942 that I discovered to some degree the fragility of human beings when the utmost is asked of them. Since then too, I have often thought that in every country in the world there must be perhaps roughly the same proportion of human beings who when the worst is asked of them will do it.' This time Roger remained in Switzerland.

Brother Roger was undoubtedly deeply hurt by this experience of denunciation and violence, but he was aware of the dangers of reaction. Again he called upon the insights of his childhood. He had seen his father regret the leniency with which he had treated his elder children and therefore handle Roger with a severity that was difficult to justify in any terms other than those of reaction. Once more Brother Roger determined not to react but to consent. Nor would he, he resolved, founder under the burden of despair at the prospect of injustice and suffering and so offer humanity his sadness instead of the inner joy available to every Christian. Compelled to remain in Switzerland, he continued the thrice daily prayer in a side chapel of the cathedral in Geneva, together with members of the Grande Communauté and with two young men who were subsequently to become the first brothers.

During 1941, in the Cluny House at Taizé, Roger had written an eighteen-page pamphlet in which he outlined briefly his monastic ideal for a life of communion. 'The very first version I compiled for my own benefit. Whilst I was still young I had realized that I would need a point of reference on which to build, references taken from the Gospels which spoke powerfully to me. Without something very central to which I would return throughout my life, how would I ever develop myself within? It was not that I wanted to make some sort of system out of a few words taken primarily from the Beatitudes because it was the Beatitudes that spoke to me most, but that I hoped to create a little inner unity. If it was going to be a question of taking great risks for God and for Christ – and it was risks and not ease I hoped for – there would be a need to keep a watch on myself, to refer to something which throughout my life would be a point of reference, something constantly to return to. That was all.'

'There are', asserts Brother Roger, 'some texts in the Scriptures which are more fundamental than others. I have always considered the Beatitudes to be essential texts and so, when it came to writing something down, I began with the three words that encapsulated the spirit of the Beatitudes: joy, simplicity and mercy. In them was the essential of the gospel.'

With the passage of time, however, Roger came to recognize the need for a more collective point of reference, 'a communal source by which a parable of community might be realized on a daily basis'. As the conclusion of their studies drew near for many of the students who had taken part in the discussion, prayer and retreats Roger had instigated, the 'solitude', the 'state of isolation' that threatened to reduce their enthusiasm and commitment to the desire for a quiet life once they were called upon to pursue their separate paths, seems to have impelled Roger to work out more explicitly the basis for a life in community which would 'use to the full the riches engendered by collaboration'. In order to do this he sought amongst the great traditions of those who had shared the same ideal and, since it was a Christian community that he wished to form, he looked primarily to Christian traditions in an attempt to form a community living in the world, a community each member of which would be bound by his faith in Christ and by certain rules. It would also be a community which, confronted by all the distress in the world of the twentieth century, would 'follow the example of those who, in the darker periods of the past when humanity was passing through great upheavals, gathered together with the same desire for silence, meditation and the dedication of their lives in order better to serve the kingdom of their Lord, and by this service to provide succour for a number of people.' The community's maxim was the ancient Benedictine maxim of 'oraet labora', prayer and work, to which was added the two words 'ut regnet' to emphasize the ultimate aim of both prayer and work and hence the spirit in which they should be undertaken. 'Prayer and work are in the service of the

46

Kingdom. They are dominated by the vision of the reign of Christ,' proclaimed the pamphlet which Brother Roger published in 1941. It also outlined three rules: the first – 'that in your day, work and rest be quickened by the word of God' – emphasized that prayer and meditation must quicken not only the moments consecrated to it but the entire day; the second – 'keep inner silence in all things that you may dwell in Christ' – drew attention to the fact that inner silence was nonetheless not to be an end in itself, not merely an emptying of the mind but rather the striving for that condition of which St John speaks, which is indispensable to those who wish to dwell in Christ. The third rule was an invitation to 'be filled with the spirit of the Beatitudes: the joy that is afforded by Christian freedom and the promises of the gospel, mercy in a world of mounting hatred, and simplicity in your way of life and in your most profound attitude, the kind of simplicity which strives for a renunciation of the self'.

Some of what was outlined in these explanatory notes was later to be altered. In 1944, Brother Roger published a booklet entitled *Introduction to Community Life* which developed his initial notes, but he soon allowed it to go out of print. His thinking was evolving rapidly, and in many respects, after only a few years, this first book no longer corresponded with his vision. The actual *Rule of Taizé*, in which Brother Roger describes for his brothers the essential aspects of their common life, was not committed to paper until the winter of 1952–3, and that too would be subsequently modified and simplified. But it is perhaps significant to note that the essence of what was to come was already present in an explanatory pamphlet compiled by a young man twenty-five years old, who had yet to complete his studies, and published with the assistance of the Abbé Couturier in Lyon, who was a poioneer of ecumenism. Among those who read the pamphlet were

47

two other students who were later to become the first two brothers. Max Thurian was studying theology and Pierre Souvairan was reading agriculture when they responded to Roger's publication and came to join him in a flat that belonged to his family in the shadow of Geneva's imposing cathedral. There they were joined by a fourth, Daniel de Montmollin, and together they embarked upon a life of common work and prayer, committing themselves provisionally to celibacy and community of material possessions with a promise that would be renewed annually. Max was preparing a dissertation on liturgy and Roger returned to his uncompleted thesis on a subject not entirely unrelated to what was beginning to take shape within him, 'The ideal of the monastic life before St Benedict and its conformity to the Gospels'. Roger successfully defended the work on 30 April 1943 and with it the concept that it was possible to live a monastic life and still remain faithful to the gospel, a suggestion which was not greeted with unqualified warmth in Protestant circles. In the same year Roger was ordained a pastor, a step which after a few years he would look back upon with some embarrassment as being in some way 'unnecessary', preferring to be a brother and nothing more.

'In truth,' recalls Brother Roger, 'a common life, a very beautiful life began very quickly in Geneva on the basis of that little pamphlet.' The flat was always full of people; so too was the side chapel they used in the cathedral. His sister Geneviève, who played the organ for the service, remembers her own surprise at the large number of people who came to join in the prayer, before they went to work in the morning. She also remembers the surprised response of some to the discovery that candles were illuminated for the duration of the service. They were taken aback, she reflects, because candles meant Roman Catholicism.

3

TOWARDS COMMUNITY

'Reconciliation', asserts Brother Roger, 'was there from the very beginning, reconciliation in the common life, "That they all may be one; as thou, Father, art in me, and I in thee, that they also may be one in us" [John 17.21] – reconciliation between Christians, reconciliation between man and his fellow men.' It was an objective which was to be put to the test in a very concrete fashion in the autumn of 1944. With the liberation of France Roger and his three prospective brothers moved to the house at Taizé in the conviction that they must continue with the venture of having amongst them 'those who were most bereft'. Who, however, would be the most bereft in the human desert where they were to settle? The answer was presented to them when it was decided that German prisoners of war should be installed in the abandoned villages very close to Taizé: some at Mont, others in a former youth camp near Chazelles. The small community obtained permission to visit the prisoner-of-war camps and there they discovered that those in charge of the German prisoners were in terms of their humanity 'the poorest of the poor'.

The plight of the occupants of the camps touched the young men at Taizé deeply. They shared with the afflicted prisoners the little food that was available at the time and on Sundays they were permitted to receive a number of them at the house for a meal and a brief moment of prayer. To have known the two situations, that of the political refugees, those who were hiding, those who were seeking refuge, and then very shortly afterwards that of the German prisoners of war who were 'just as innocent as the first', remains for Brother Roger a powerful experience. His sympathy and compassion were not, however, shared by all of the local population. Some of the men from the area around Taizé who belonged to the Resistance had never returned from their secret activities. There were feelings of vengeance on the part of two or three of the women, and hatred engendered hatred. One day some of the women whose husbands had been deported and died in German concentration camps set upon one young prisoner with leather harnesses used for cattle. Weak and undernourished as he was, he died of the beating, but he was a priest and in his last hours he expressed only peace and forgiveness. 'For some time previously,' Brother Roger recalls, 'I had noticed in him a reflection of the sanctity of God.' The experience lives on for him as a bitter-sweet memory which was to gain renewed poignance when he was able to relate it years later to a gathering of a new generation of Germans in Frankfurt.

Another story cited by the community as an inspiration to reconciliation relates to the grandmother of one of the brothers who took his final vows in 1984. Her husband was a high-ranking German military officer, who resisted and stood by his faith. The Nazi regime imprisoned him in a Gestapo prison. The woman had two children, a daughter who became the mother of the Taizé brother and a son who was killed in the war. During the war mother and daughter were forced to go into hiding separately because they were wanted by the police. Yet after the death of her son that mother was able to give expression to her feelings in lines which were read aloud on the occasion of her grandson's profession:

When I was yet a child, my mother's hand held me along all the ways, the paths, all through the wondrous land of childhood. And her hand was warm, good, firm, like a hand that would never let go.

Later there came my own child, with his child's hand that he hid in his mother's hand. And my hand held his firmly, like a hand that would never let him go.

Yet death came! It does not ask for what is readily released. And its hand is cold and grips firmly.

If now your hands are empty because of death, do not clench your fist, or God cannot make good your loss. And if he does not do so now, in our time, he will surely do it in his eternity.

This was the spirit the small community at Taizé endeavoured to foster amongst the local villagers during the harsh years that followed the liberation, for where compassion is lost, insists Brother Roger, everything is lost. The task was by no means easy. Geneviève recalls, with some humour, the antagonism of one Catholic neighbour towards the Protestant newcomers to Taizé. Such was his hostility that when the brothers' goats strayed into his garden a law-suit was threatened. The threats were dissolved by Geneviève's own sense of the comic when she found herself reduced to scrambling after the animals in a vain attempt to return them to their home ground, but a certain atmosphere of reserve prevailed. 'The beginning was not easy,' recalls Brother Roger. 'I look back on them as difficult years. We were so far from everyone, so isolated, so unfindable.' Communication was still difficult. Even visits to Macon meant a journey that took considerable time by bicycle, or on foot when bicycle tyres were beyond repair and could not be replaced. Food had to be obtained, at least for those staying with the community, on the black market and times were generally hard materially and financially. 'We have had such difficulties of that kind in our lives, yet', Brother Roger marvels, 'there has not been an occasion on which we have run out of bread – very nearly but not quite. There was one time when we had the idea of transferring all the money we had, which was not very much, to France. This had to be done by legal means, in other words, I think, through the consul in Geneva to Paris. In Paris security bonds were bought for safety reasons and they were sent here, but at that time I happened to be away in Switzerland. A big fat envelope arrived but it was not accepted because I was not here to sign for it.' For some days it remained at the Post Office until an employee intervened for someone to sign in Brother Roger's place. The envelope finally arrived and was opened, only to reveal that it was full of newspaper cuttings. That evening the brothers knew that their material resources were at an end. 'By this time everything had been liquidated. The farm was not working. Nothing was working. There was a little milk and that was all. Max had sprained his ankle and could not walk, so I put him in a little cart and took him to the Post Office several kilometres away. The postman swore blind that he had not taken it. We asked him at least to give us back part of it because we needed it. We told him he had nothing to fear from us. We would never press charges, but silence – it wasn't he who had done it.'

Despite recommendations from the judge at Cluny that all the money could be regained, Roger remained true to his word, and made no formal complaint. Yet the house at Taizé survived. 'We held out, tightened our belts as much as possible, in a way that we have had to do on many other occasions.' In order to safeguard their spiritual freedom and integrity, the brothers at Taizé have never accepted gifts or legacies. Even today the brothers' personal inheritances are not accepted by the community. All the brothers consider it essential that they live only by their own labours. It was a resolution which was particularly difficult to maintain, however, at a time when conditions in general were so harsh that many people were reduced to theft. On one occasion even the washing disappeared from the house. There were nonetheless compensations. To get up in the middle of the night to deliver a calf, for example, was an experience which Brother Roger found 'captivating'.

It was at this time of material deprivation that even greater demands were made upon the community's limited resources. Yet it was a demand which Brother Roger was able to view rather as the emergence of 'another possibility'. The war years had left many children in the area either orphaned or abandoned, or simply un-wanted. 'We took some of the boys in. But then who would take care of them? Who would be a mother to them? My youngest sister. All my other sisters were mar-ried apart from her, and I don't think it would have been long before she married if she had not come here. She, who was such a good pianist, who was an artist to the very tips of her fingers, who did not have a specially developed practical sense, took it upon herself to bring up those children here in very difficult conditions.' So it was that

Geneviève set up home with the children, initially in the neighbouring village of Masilly until an old house in the village of Taizé had been fitted out for them not far from the brothers' home. The task was an enormous one and one which Geneviève was compelled to undertake without any female assistance. Disturbed by the harshness of their early experience of life, the boys were too daunting a prospect for some to take on, but Geneviève welcomed them. If she gave them her best, her brother assured her, the boys might not realize it immediately, perhaps not welcome it at once, but ultimately it would penetrate. It would be given to them for ever and they would rediscover it in the future.

The prediction was to prove itself not without foundation. Taizé had gained an extended family, 'a discreet family' about which not too much is made public in order to safeguard something of the intimacy of an ordinary family. The adopted boys have gone their separate ways now and have their own children, for whom Geneviève is a grandmother. 'I think that I can say that they have all married well,' concludes Brother Roger. To him it is a small page in the life of Taizé which counts because it contributed so much. 'Nothing is given in the life in God without reciprocity. That is a reality which is very close to my heart. And I think that the beginning of our life together was greatly supported by the presence of those abandoned children who had only us.'

It was sustained too by the capacity for laughter. 'It's true that, being few, very few in number, we were able to survive many moments that were not easy by resorting very quickly to laughter. Laughter had an important role to play and it took very little to spark if off – even during the common prayer. Not for a single day did we doubt that our life in community was possible, but nothing happened as expected. There was no one among us with experience; so we made the most monumental mistakes.'

Confronted with the poverty of means which Roger saw as a mainspring of creativity, Charles Schutz was concerned for his son's welfare. It was not that he was entirely unsympathetic to what Roger was trying to do. He visited Taizé during the first years when Roger was there alone, was full of understanding for the work with the refugees and recognized that something must follow. Roger would have liked to discuss with him the nature of what that 'something' was to be, but he appears to have found it almost impossibly difficult. Acceptance of a life governed by what amounted to the traditional monastic vows, and in particular by celibacy, exceeded the limits of even Charles Schutz's openness of heart. For others the Protestant pastor might well have been able to accept it but not for his own son. One concession on the part of his father remains with Brother Roger. In his unfaltering love for the poor, Charles Schutz had praised the fact that historically religious orders had been responsible for educating those who could not otherwise have afforded it. He had seen a good deal of the first brothers while they were living in Geneva, but his assessment of them did not seem to allay his fears. In 1940 with a rare display of emotion he warned Roger: 'When you are old you will be alone. Those men will abandon you.' He then did something which he had never before done in front of his son. Roger had been taught since he was a very small child that a boy did not cry, but at that moment his father wept and said, 'You see your mother, what a companion she is to me.' Instantly Roger countered the suggestion: supposing his mother died before his father, the pastor too would know solitude. The older man sobbed at his table until his wife appeared and immediately appeased him.

Five years later Charles Schutz was a very sick man. He was suffering from what appears to have been a form of thrombosis and could no longer walk. For a week he was treated with leeches, which naturally weakened him. Then he caught pneumonia and was directed to remain in bed but, determined to get up, he persuaded his wife to help him to a chair. Weak and enveloped in blankets, he chose at last to talk to his son. He talked about dependence, about the importance of being financially sufficient in order to be free, and that night Roger did try to explain to his father his aspirations. 'After you have raised the stock, and cultivated the land, that will certainly not be enough,' were Charles Schutz's last words to his son. Having expressed his very practical concern he was put back to bed, slipped into a coma and died.

This conversation, because it was his last with a father whose reactions, by Brother Roger's own admission, counted for far more than those of all the rest of Protestantism, was to leave an indelible impression upon him.

Despite Charles Schutz's predictions, and to Brother Roger's evident joy, all of the first brothers are with him still. By 1947 also, thanks to the agricultural skills of one of the brothers, the community which from the very earliest days had endeavoured to support itself by its own labours, was producing enough to become relatively stable financially. It also provided a welcome for a steady flow of visitors, among them not only Catholic priests and religious but also Protestant theologians for whom the common prayer of a twentieth-century monastic community was of special interest. Furthermore, there were the gatherings of the Grande Communauté, although in 1950 this idea was abandoned. Its members, it was felt, were becoming self-sufficient, too detached from their local communities and in danger of being regarded as some form of independent church movement. There was also a feeling that the development of two projects, that of the community at Taizé and the Grande Communauté was inappropriate, and so their meetings were brought to an end. Nevertheless, the upper room in the brothers' house which had been set aside as a chapel was filled to overflowing.

Meanwhile the small Roman church in the village of Taizé stood empty and virtually unused. Since the French Revolution only the funerals of the villagers had been conducted there. There was no parish priest and, since Brother Roger had come to Taizé, there had been only one Mass celebrated in the neglected building: the Abbé Couturier, a pioneer of Christian unity whom Brother Roger had met in 1940 and a man who was to become a close friend of the community, had come to visit Brother Roger and celebrated the first Mass there for many years. Accordingly Brother Roger sought permission to use the village church: 'We were praying in a room and everything was very cramped. But that was not the most important question. What mattered was that the little church was secularized and we wanted it to be once more a place of prayer.' For Brother Roger there is a special attraction to those places in which there has been a long tradition of prayer, 'perhaps because in them the faith of the Church has been confirmed by the centuries'. With the consent of the local dean, the Abbé Dutroncy, the brothers began to use the village church for their daily prayer. 'We arranged things a little and went there to pray morning, noon and night. Then, a few weeks later, we received a visit in the course of which we were asked not to go there any more. We realized, therefore, that we must give up. Time passed and we knew that only the bishop could take up the issue again. Taizé is in the archdiocese of Lyon and the diocese of Autun, which is a very large diocese and we are in the antipodes. A mountain separates us from Autun itself.' Nevertheless, when Brother Roger eventually met the Bishop of Autun he seemed to understand and, although somewhat nervous and reluctant himself to take the responsibility for granting so unusual a request, he did refer the matter to a higher authority. At Whitsun 1948 the village church was made available for the brothers' common prayer by a *simultaneum*, a system by which in parts of France the Catholic authorities may agree to the additional use of a Catholic church building for Protestant services, and the authorization was signed by Angelo Giuseppe Roncalli, then papal nuncio in Paris but subsequently to become Pope John XXIII, 'that man of so large a heart' who was to place such immense trust in Taizé and so to have such a significant role to play in the development of the community.

So it was in the little Romanesque village church, at Easter 1949, that the first seven brothers took the three traditional monastic vows, committing themselves for life to celibacy, to community of goods, and the acceptance of an authority represented by the figure of the prior. During the previous year three young Frenchmen, one of whom was a doctor, had visited Taizé and chosen to remain. The new arrivals had accentuated the need to confront a constantly recurring question as to whether their commitment should remain a provisional one. To Brother Roger there is energy in the provisional, a dynamic in the movement away from static traditions in the direction of continuous flexibility. 'We tried not to let ourselves be unduly influenced by the experience of others. We wanted to start anew. In spite of this,' he concedes, 'one day it became apparent to us that we could not remain faithful to our vocation without committing ourselves with the three vows.' Thus it was that, with few witnesses from the outside world, the ancient monastic ideal became a reality amongst men who issued from the Churches of the Reformation.

Asked to pinpoint what, in view of a commitment which is common to so many religious orders, is specific to

Taizé, Brother Roger responds: 'I think reconciliation.' Reconciliation, which his grandmother had not talked about but which she had actually lived and realized. 'She was not to be followed by her three sons but that did not matter. What mattered was that she accomplished it without being rejected, and without ever professing to anyone to have found a solution.'

Entry into the community was not always a step devoid of family complications. The profession of two brothers from the same family took place in 1949 and 1950. Their father was one of those men of 'inner understanding' who was to provide the inspiration needed for the small community to continue. It was feared, however, that their mother would not be able to accept her sons' vocations in the same way. For a while, therefore, to spare her pain one of the brothers would remove his ring whenever he visited his mother. Inevitably the day came when he forgot to do so. Some time later, however, in response to another visitor's comment that she had a son in the community, the same mother was heard to remark with pride that she had two. The experience is one which can now be looked back upon with joy.

With the more permanent establishment of the Taizé community, contact with other churches could more easily be undertaken. The least motion to draw closer to other Christian traditions was to remain nevertheless a sensitive and complex undertaking. Following Angelo Roncalli's intervention, the Bishop of Autun had the reassuring knowledge that he was not without authoritative support in permitting the use of the village church for the brothers' prayer. 'From then on we saw more and more of him. He lost some of his timidity and became a good bishop to us.' Nevertheless, some of the Bishop of Autun's apprehensions with regard to the reaction of the Holy Office were to remain until the Second Vatican

Council. Not until then would he himself come to take part in the brothers' prayer in the little church, and if a Catholic wished to join the community in prayer a specific request had to be made to him, a process which was so complicated that sometimes the brothers did not dare pursue it. For a time they found themselves in what seemed to them the extraordinary situation of having to close the doors in case Catholics should venture in during the common prayer. Then there was also the question of an ecumenical meeting of monks and priests from Holland which the brothers would have liked to be held at Taizé. Again their request was referred to the papal nuncio in Paris. On this occasion, however, they received no response. The time was evidently not yet right. These things, it was accepted, could not be forced.

Their understanding was to be further put to the test when Brother Roger showed the Bishop of Autun a prayer which he had written and placed on the seats of the village church in order that those who came there might use it. Without consulting the author, the bishop took the initiative of sending the prayer to the Holy Office, which meant that a meeting of the Holy Office was held on the subject. Unwanted attention was thus drawn to the fact that the community was using the village church for prayer and, after a vote, it was resolved that the brothers should be permitted to continue but that in consequence the Catholic Mass would no longer be permitted to be celebrated there. The Bishop of Autun was directed to make an announcement to that effect in every church in the diocese. For those whose hearts were set on reconciliation it must have seemed a cruel act of rejection, and the bishop was so tormented by the outcome of his intervention that he came to Brother Roger and expressed his intention of leaving his office. Anxious that too much should not be made of the incident, the Prior of Taizé urged him not to

'lose the peace of Christ without which all else is lost'.
'Nevertheless,' concedes Brother Roger, 'it did touch me
very much, but if there was no other way we must remain
silent and not make too much of a story out of it.'

Fortunately, there were others in the archdiocese who
were quick to recognize and identify with Taizé's search
for means of reconciliation between Christians. The Abbé
Couturier, who had been one of the first to stimulate
prayer for unity in Lyon, a city which vigorously supported ecumenism, swiftly established contact between
the Prior of Taizé and the Archbishop of Lyon, Cardinal
Gerlier, a man whose openness and foresight had made
the prevailing enthusiasm for reconciliation possible. 'The
Cardinal was already an old man, but he was the first
churchman to have confidence in us, and it was he who
first had the idea that I should go to Rome.' In 1948 the
World Council of Churches had been set up in Amster-
dam. The response from the Holy Office at that time was,
however, far from encouraging. In June of that year it
published a text which effectively forbade Catholic participation in ecumenical meetings. At Lyon, this text
was deeply regretted and so too was the treatment of
certain more forward-looking theologians within the
archdiocese. It was with these issues in mind that
Cardinal Gerlier suggested that Brother Roger should go
to Rome to establish direct contact with Pope Pius XII and
to talk to him about ecumenism. He also arranged for
Brother Roger to have audiences with four men who,
the Cardinal considered, might give him a sympathetic
hearing: with Father Boyer who was responsible to the
Pope for ecumenism, with Monsignor Ottaviani in the
Holy Office, with Pizzardo the Cardinal president, and
with Montini, the then Under-Secretary of State and the
future Pope Paul VI. 'That was our beloved Cardinal Gerlier,' reflects Brother Roger, 'a man of initiatives, of

suggestions, of intuitions, who opened the way for us. It would never have occurred to me to go and speak.'

At the Cardinal's instigation, however, Brother Roger and Brother Max boarded the train for Rome. 'And it was unutterably wonderful because Monsignor Montini understood everything. We had two meetings with Monsignor Montini and it was from that time that a spiritual friendship began.' Montini advised Brother Roger not to approach the Pope at a doctrinal or theological level because Pius XII was a theologian and had a very precise viewpoint, but he was also a pastor and at that level he would listen. Brother Roger should therefore try to touch his pastoral heart. At that first audience Brother Roger sought to convey to Pope Pius XII the entreaty, 'Leave a little way open, even a very narrow one and define what you consider to be the essential barriers – but leave a way forward. Do not close it altogether'. The appeal did not go totally without response, for in the following year the Holy Office produced another text which was written in a rather different tone from the previous one and which did indeed leave certain openings, in that it granted to local bishops the responsibility for deciding whether Catholics within the diocese should take part in ecumenical activities.

The relationship between the community at Taizé and the ageing Cardinal Gerlier was to be sustained and strengthened. 'He used to come and see us with his chauffeur Jean in a large old car, and we loved it. He was our spiritual father. He had at one time been Bishop of Lourdes and he was a very Marian man. His motto was "Ad Jesum per Mariam", and those words were inscribed everywhere about him. You could see them all over his house, and I think that the deep humanity in that man came from his understanding of Mary. If through him the Church expressed itself so maternally, not just pastorally but maternally, it was because there was in him this strong reference to the mystery of communion with Mary.' Cardinal Gerlier bore in him the same spirit of selfless giving for which Brother Roger has striven throughout the development of Taizé: 'Yesterday as today the gesture remains the same – the Virgin Mary gives that which she has received, her son, and we are called upon to give that which God entrusts to us, provisionally, here upon the hill.'

In 1950, once again at the request of Cardinal Gerlier, Brother Roger was called upon to go to Rome. 1950 was a Holy Year which Pope Pius XII was due to mark with a promulgation of the dogma of the Assumption of the Blessed Virgin Mary, and it was feared that his intended action would widen the gulf between the Catholic Church and the Churches of the Reformation. For Brother Roger there was no objection to the doctrine of the Assumption. If the Pope had made a simple declaration on the subject, his action would not have created any particular difficulties. What Brother Roger saw as so grave an obstacle to the path of reconciliation and the small beginnings made by the ecumenical movement was the proposed use of papal infallibility. The practice was due to be invoked for the first time since the First Vatican Council in 1870, when the Roman Catholic Church declared that the Pope was infallible when he defined that a doctrine concerning faith or morals was part of the deposit of divine revelation. It was Cardinal Gerlier's suggestion that if Brother Roger were to talk to the Pope he might reconsider so sensitive a point. In Rome it was again Monsignor Montini who was to give the Prior of Taizé constructive assistance and advice. Montini suggested that Brother Roger prepare a written text which he would pass on to the Pope. 'He arranged for us to be accompanied by Monsignor Veuillot who was in charge of French affairs in the Secretariat of

State, and as we passed through the rooms leading to the Pope's audience chamber, Monsignor Veuillot said to us, "Remember the Pope is an old man." He advised us to act a little upon his sensibilities, so I spoke and the Pope listened and responded. Then at a certain moment, he opened up. He had consulted bishops throughout the world as to whether he should make the promulgation and almost all of them had replied that he should. "How do you expect the promulgation not to take place," he asked me, "when more than ninety per cent replied, Yes?" Pius XII was a man of great spirituality. We venerated the face of that man, his attitude, but we were made to understand one thing – that it was too late.'

The promulgation originally arranged for August 1950 was delayed until 1 November. 'Here in Taizé we listened to the radio, waiting to hear how the promulgation would be presented. When we heard it and grasped the fact that the Pope had made use of the dogma of in-fallibility, I don't think at first we said anything.' That afternoon the eight brothers who by that time comprised the community went for a walk. The weather was grey, overcast and cheerless, and Roger said to his brothers: 'For us this is a day of mourning.' He knew that neither he nor his brothers would relinquish their passion for reconciliation, that on the contrary they would seek at once a means of continuing their quest, but he feared that many non-Catholics who had begun to be more open would now turn away from ecumenism and that the divisions between denominations would be rein-forced. Furthermore, what had occurred that day would provide those who were already firmly opposed to the Catholic Church with an additional source of argument. Sure enough, for several years the outcome was to be as predicted. 'We have known a long winter,' Brother Roger was later to say. Of Pius XII he remarks simply: 'I hardly knew him. He had something very venerable about him for he was impassioned by God, but he was less accessible than those who were to succeed him.'

4

A SPRINGTIME IN THE CHURCH

'Today we went to visit the community of Protestant brothers of Taizé . . .' So, over thirty-five years ago, wrote the foundress of the order of the Little Sisters of Jesus. 'We spent two happy hours together. They are extremely sympathetic. Their thinking is a little surprising: they want to revive the Catholic religion by their radiance in the village! Who would ever have thought such a thing possible? . . .' 'They want to go and see the Holy Father and Msgr Montini,' she added later in her letter, 'and they dream of a single Church attached to Rome.' The letter, dated 31 July 1948, provides a significant indication that even at such an early stage in the development of Taizé there was a clear intuition that the road to Christian unity passed through the reconciliation of the non-Catholic churches with the Church of Rome. Apart from any historical or theological considerations, the example of his grandmother and the natural affinities of Brother Roger's youth, it may be suggested, impelled him to seek solutions in that direction.

Perhaps inevitably such a recognition led to misunderstandings and criticisms on the part of some members of the Reformed Churches. Such criticism as has been levelled at the Taizé community has been based on the fact that its life and thinking was too close to the Catholic Church. This was not something for which Brother Roger was unprepared: 'My own father's letters of exegesis had shown me what the reaction of Protestantism would be. Yet my father had admired my grandmother so much. "She is so deep," he used to say, "She loves the poor. She has effected reconciliation in a small way."'

As soon as the promulgation of the dogma of the Assumption had been made, Brother Roger resolved that nothing should be said about what had occurred during his visit to Rome. The fact that such an appeal had been made and rejected could be divisive in its effect. Word of Brother Roger's gesture did, however, reach the ears of Pastor Marc Boegner, President of the Federation of the Protestant Churches of France, in Paris. So it came about that during a visit to him the Prior of Taizé was asked how he could conceivably have ventured to go and see the Pope in the Vatican. Boegner used harsh words and spoke of Protestant patrimony. Had Brother Roger explained the reason for his visit Boegner would have appreciated it for, as the community was later to discover, he was a man open to differing viewpoints. But Brother Roger also knew that if he were to recount what had taken place during the audience with Pius XII he would have attracted considerable sympathy to himself and thereby aroused further opposition to the Pope. The brothers had therefore agreed to remain silent on the subject, recognizing that unity is not created through opposition or division. Nevertheless, seeing Boegner's anxiety, Brother Roger sought to reassure him that his intentions were not divisive, rather the opposite. The pastor's apprehensions would appear to have been allayed. Indeed, fifteen years later Pastor Boegner was himself to meet Paul VI in Rome on several occasions. 'Those were our beginnings,' recalls Brother Roger, 'a very significant period of our existence. One must not seek to unite by dividing, nor must one try to gather sympathies about one by opposing others.'

There was a time when some French-speaking Protestant leaders sought to link Taizé more firmly to the Churches of the Reformation. Brother Roger explained to them that he could not agree to their suggestion, assuring them nonetheless that his was not a sectarian spirit, that he had no intention of creating a sect or a new separate Church. 'On several occasions we were asked to found a new Church, but a creation of that kind would have been contrary to our search for reconciliation. We do not want to renew the process of reform which consists of, ... whenever things are going badly or when there is some new inspiration, creating a new Church. Those who have created a new Church have been very fervent in the beginning but later on the same problems appeared.' The brothers have seen too much of the negative consequences of this process in Protestantism to wish to use it in their turn.

Yet if Brother Roger did not wish Taizé to become a new Church neither did he seek a static situation in which reconciliation would remain merely a theory or idea. From the very beginning he wanted the community to be a real parable of communion, a parable of reconciliation open to a future which embraced the concrete and visible unity of all Christians. If Taizé had existed solely for Protestantism the parable of community would not have been able to expand in all its dimensions, and Taizé might even have reinforced the divisions between denominations by creating a Protestant monachism parallel to the Catholic and Orthodox monasticism. 'We are here,' states Brother Roger, 'because of Christ and the gospel, and Christ has in a sense called us to recapture the image of a reconciled Church. That is the point of the vocation of the Taizé community. There is this wounded Christ whom we wish to follow in the unique communion that is his body, whom we do not wish to abandon. We wish to be a small reflection of what that communion is for everyone, a small reflection of the Church that is constantly reconciling itself.' To Brother Roger, who has said that he would not know how to pray without his body, the idea of the association of spirit and body applies as much to Christ and the universal Church as it does to humanity. Thus to love Christ is to love his Church and if the Church is torn and suffering, there is all the more reason not to desert it.

Outside on the grass beneath the trees, where visitors may sit and talk with members of the community, an Italian brother recounted a dream to me. Around us as he spoke young people were seated with the brothers in pairs or small groups, sheltering from the sun and engaged in earnest conversation. 'While Brother Roger was in Rome on one occasion,' the brother told me, 'I dreamt that a large number of the brothers, including Brother Roger, were in a city which I thought I recognized as Rome. We had gathered around a fountain surrounded by red flowers in a very pretty square. Suddenly an old woman appeared. She was dressed all in black and had a red face covered with wrinkles like a southern Italian woman. In her arms she was carrying a child. He was a little boy of two or three but he had no hair and his arms and legs were disproportionately long. She gave this child to Brother Roger who began to cover him with kisses. The woman explained that he was sick and that he had been born like that. When someone asked our brother why he was embracing such an ugly child, he replied, 'Because it is he'. When we turned round to give the child back to his mother, she had disappeared. All that day I asked myself what that dream might signify, and on the next night I had another dream or perhaps it was a continuation of the first: Brother Roger was due back from Rome. The brothers had all assembled, as we do when he returns from a journey. When he came in he embraced us all but it was apparent that the meetings in Rome had not gone well. Before the icon in the corner of his room he said: "What God asks of us and grants to us is to have the passion not to leave his Christ who is suffering for his torn Church. That is our vocation." The dreams came at a time', the brother added, 'when there were special difficulties within the Church.' Were dreams important to Brother Roger? They seemed to hold a certain reality for him. 'Only,' replied the brother, 'from the point of view that he believes that, as in the gospel, we should take note of the signs that are given to us. They may perhaps be taken as a suggestion that we should give a little more thought to something.' There came to mind another dream among a number which Brother Roger himself has recorded, a dream in which someone invisible placed in his hands a figure of Christ and so evoked from him an expression of joy. The details of his own words eluded him but that was not important. It was, he says, enough for him to know that Christ is close to him.

Whatever the interpretation or importance attributed to dreams, the brother's words provided a sensitive visual metaphor of Brother Roger's enduring love for the afflicted Church that is the body of Christ, a love and a vision which, in the days of what was known as the winter of ecumenism, was to add another dimension to the risk he was called to take in following the road opened by his elderly grandmother. How could he continue without further wounding the suffering body of Christ?

'Christ calumniated said nothing in reply,' reminds Brother Roger. It was an example he had learnt to emulate from childhood. 'All my life when people have taken me to task I have struggled to remain silent.' He had learnt too that he must consent and not react, and also has learnt the importance of what he calls 'spiritual tact'. There can be little doubt, however, that at times the breakdown of communication between members of different denominations has caused him great personal suffering. The question as to what has been among his greatest trials wrests from him a fleeting sigh of sadness, not recrimination: 'The failure of churchmen to understand the essential of what we are trying to live'. There were, he concedes, times in the beginning when he found communication easier with those who were not churchmen and times also when his intentions were misrepresented or disfigured.

In the years 1952, 1954 and 1955, representatives from Taizé were invited to attend ecumenical meetings in Rome, but Brother Roger refers, without criticism, to those years as a period in which there was a certain 'emptiness'. In 1958 Pius XII died, having privately expressed his regret that he had not concerned himself sufficiently with ecumenism. In public he had also forecast 'a springtime of the Church'. As far as Taizé was concerned the election of Pius XII's successor was certainly to mark the beginning of a new and vital phase in the community's relationship with the Church of Rome. Once again it was Cardinal Gerlier who was to be the instigator of that relationship. John XXIII was virtually unknown to the brothers at Taizé, although they were of course aware that it was he who had authorized the *simultaneum* for the use of the village church. There was some surprise within the community, therefore, at the election of a man so advanced in years and so comparatively unknown. Immediately after news of the election of Angelo Roncalli had reached the world, Cardinal Gerlier, in an audience granted even before the papal enthronement, appealed to the new Pope on two counts. Cardinal Gerlier was a year older than John XXIII, and said to him: 'I shall die before you [a suggestion which was not in fact to prove the case] and I would like to leave my testament to you. I have two preoccupations to entrust to you: the first is greater justice for mankind and the second is ecumenism. With regard to ecumenism I would like you to agree to see the Taizé brothers immediately.' 'Like me, the Pope is an old man,' Cardinal Gerlier explained later, 'and when you are old you forget many things. It was, therefore, important that he should have an immediate impression before he became caught up in a multitude of other considerations.'

So persuasive was the Cardinal that John XXIII eventually agreed to receive the brothers but only on one condition, namely that they did not ask him questions that were too difficult. The Cardinal accordingly despatched a telegram summoning Brother Roger to Rome where he and Brother Max were given careful instructions. It was considered imperative that they should have a private audience at which they would be able to have the opportunity to speak at some length. If, therefore, they found themselves in a particular room in the Vatican which was allocated to those destined for an audience at which visitors merely filed past the Pope and had a brief exchange, they were directed to withdraw immediately. Cardinal Gerlier would then initiate proceedings again, a task which would be almost impossible once Brother Roger had accepted a briefer form of meeting. As it transpired no such difficulties presented themselves. 'The audience', recalls Brother

Roger, 'happened just as Cardinal Gerlier had wished. Three days after the inauguration we were summoned and there we were before the Pope. That audience with John XXIII was a little surprising because he was so different from everything that we had imagined. He was so interested and when we spoke of reconciliation he clapped his hands and exclaimed "Bravo". He was such a simple man, so open, so full of joy and spontaneity.' So spontaneous was he in fact that the thought passed fleetingly through Brother Roger's mind that this might not after all be the Pope he was addressing. 'From that very first meeting a bond was established between them,' another brother recounts, 'a bond that came from the heart at a level that could not really be rationally grasped.' Brother Roger had encountered 'a man like Cardinal Gerlier, a man of faith who inspired confidence and made us welcome'. 'That audience', he remembers, 'gave a new stimulus to our ecumenical endeavours. From then onwards Pope John had an unexpected influence on us and, without knowing it, let a little springtime be born for Taizé.' Nor was Brother Roger's conviction that something exceptional had occurred during that first meeting unreciprocated. Monsignor Capovilla, John XXIII's secretary, heard the Pope remark afterwards that the encounter had been a special experience for him. John XXIII's parting comments to Brother Roger included an expression of profound interest and an invitation to return. From that time onwards a meeting of a similar kind was to take place annually. The Church of Rome had assumed a more open and welcoming face.

Only months later, on 25 January 1959, Pope John XXIII announced his intention of convening an ecumenical council for the Church to which were invited a number of non-Roman Catholic observers. Among these guests were Brother Roger and one of his brothers from Taizé. The invitation and the spirit which inspired it did not fail to call forth a positive response. This new-found confidence meant that a text compiled for the forthcoming Second Vatican Council could express Taizé's hopes for it unequivocally and with urgency:

> Recognizing clearly the scandal of the separations existing between us who are all Christians, we are in quest of a visible unity. It and it alone can render possible an outburst of mission capable of bringing the glad news of the gospel to every person in the world ... We know that the Catholic Church maintains that she has preserved intact the unity desired by Christ. It is not for us to judge that conviction. But it must be said that the manner in which that unity is affirmed is frequently hurtful for those Christians who are not Catholic. When the Catholic Church expresses the goal of Christian unity in terms such as 'returning to the fold' or 'submitting' to her, dialogue at once becomes impossible. Surely it would be possible to employ terms implying a 'common advance towards' or 'together fulfilling' total unity? Otherwise, there can be no real dialogue ... Protestantism needs repeated declarations of the kind made by the Pope, 'We will not put history on trial. We will not try to establish who was right and who was wrong. Responsibilities lie on both sides. All we shall say is: Let us unite! Let us put an end to disagreements!'

A voice was beginning to make itself heard from Taizé, although it was a voice which the community was ever anxious to prevent from appearing authoritarian, inflexible or judgemental. 'It was not in the strong wind or the earthquake that God spoke to Elijah but in a still, small voice [1 Kings 19]. God, the Holy Spirit, speaks to us all, not in violence,' reminds Brother Roger, 'but in that still small voice.' The appeal for reconciliation did not go entirely unheeded. In September 1960, and again in September of the following year, Brother Roger invited a dozen Catholic bishops and approximately fifty Protestant pastors to meet at Taizé for three days. The gathering that ensued was the first of its kind to take place since the Reformation, and in order that those present should not dwell on the divisions of the past Brother Roger invited them rather to share with one another the common pastoral concerns each was experiencing in the contemporary world. In particular he drew their attention to the situation in Latin America, a situation about which at the time Europe showed little concern. A few days after the second of these meetings, yet another unprecedented event was to take place: Cardinal Gerlier and Pastor Boegner met at Taizé for a day of reflection with the community.

Within the context of an increasing awareness of changing tides of scepticism about and enthusiasm for ecumenism in the Church as a whole, the life of communion and prayer at Taizé seemed to Brother Roger all the more important as a means of creating continuity and of becoming what he sees as a 'living rock'. This was not to be a continuity provided by rigid discipline or unnecessary austerity. Even *The Rule of Taizé* which he had written in the course of a silent retreat during the winter of 1952–3 carefully avoided the use of any direct expression of obligation. At that time it was the general practice for religious communities to have a Rule, but even then Brother Roger had been concerned that formalism should not set in. It did not specify, for example, such details as how the brothers should spend their day, or what they should wear or even how their prayer should be conducted, but concentrated only on what was considered to be truly essential for a common life shared by men in their inalienable freedom, and on that which, it was hoped, would make the community not merely a juxtapositioning of individuals but creators together. In this common life the regular, thrice daily prayer brought rhythm and renewed resources, resources upon which steadily increasing demands were being made.

Shortly after the election of Pope John XXIII the decision made by the Holy Office with regard to the use of the Roman church in Taizé was reversed. By a new vote the brothers were once more granted the unconditional use of it. By the late 1950s, however, the little church could no longer contain the people who were beginning to flock to the Sunday services at Taizé not only from France, but also from Switzerland, Germany, England and Holland. The brothers' primary welcome was a welcome to prayer. There could be no question of turning away the growing number of young people who had begun to come in order to join in the common prayer, but Brother Roger admits that their advent, like the role of Taizé in the world at large, was something for which he had not been prepared and with which he at first found difficulty coping. 'What I had envisaged was a small group, a few men bound for life by a commitment to a life in God, a life of prayer, a contemplative life but who would work – and who would not look for anything else. We could never have imagined all that was to follow.' To his first brothers Brother Roger had even one day confided that they would confine the community to twelve. Yet that early vision was already being eroded. At first it was thought that a meeting place for young people could be made out of a disused chapel four kilometres away; the brothers were understandably reluctant to allow themselves to be submerged by too many people. Then it was thought that on summer Sundays a solution might be found by erecting a roof or hangar which would provide shelter from the sun and the rain, and which the brothers could construct themselves.

Gradually it had become apparent that they were being called upon to live the parable of community in a much wider context and 'in a certain transparency'.

It was at this juncture that a German organization known as 'Sühnezeichen', which had been founded after the war by German Christians to construct signs of reconciliation in places of war-time suffering, sent representatives to Taizé. Recognizing an all too obvious need, they offered to raise the funds and provide a volunteer workforce to construct a new church as a sign of reconciliation. Taizé had always had a special relationship with Germans, perhaps because of its early relationship with the German prisoners of war. Sühnezeichen had chosen the village as the site of a sign of reconciliation between Germany and France and so, almost despite himself, Brother Roger found himself agreeing to the construction of a building which he had for some time opposed. 'One of the brothers is an architect and as part of his final course he wanted to design a church for Taizé. I had told him, "If the project interests you by all means design a church, but you must know that a church will never be built at Taizé. We are not going to construct buildings. We are not builders." His project was well received and when it was decided that we would, after all, construct something, I was shown the little models. They looked tiny but they would provide for summer Sundays. Then one day I returned to find high pillars and a roof in the process of being built and I realized that we were doing something much bigger than I had supposed.'

The Church of Reconciliation was built by a team of young Germans who at the end of a day's labouring on the construction site would wash, change and appear in the little village church to join the brothers for evening prayer. At the same time the brothers began to prepare themselves to build a place in which the visiting young people could be made welcome. 'What we had opened four kilometres away was totally unrealistic. Those four kilometres in a life of common prayer were impossible.' By July 1962 the new church was nearing completion. It was decided, therefore, that its inauguration would be celebrated on the approaching Feast of the Transfiguration. 'The whole vision of the transfiguration of man made its impression on me from the very beginning, perhaps because of Peter the Venerable, the twelfth-century Abbot of Cluny who introduced to Cluny and thus to the Western Church a feast that originated in the East. That feast found a great deal of resonance in us. We look upon it above all as the celebration of that presence of Christ which takes charge of everything in us and transfigures even that which disturbs us about ourselves. God penetrates those hardened, incredulous, even disquieting regions within us, about which we really do not know what to do. He penetrates them with the life of his Spirit, and when he penetrates them he acts upon those regions and gives them his face. He traverses them to give them his face – he transfigures.'

This was the light in which Brother Roger viewed the celebrations of 5–7 August 1962 which, not insignificantly, were to assemble an ecumenical gathering unprecedented in the history of the Christian Church. Some members of the Central Committee of the World Council of Churches were present, Pastor Marc Boegner came as president of the Federation of Protestant Churches of France and Bishop Kurt Scharf as president of the German Evangelical Churches. Bishop Martin of Rouen represented the Catholic Church, Metropolitan Meliton attended as representative of the Patriarch of Constantinople and Bishop Oliver Tomkins was the special envoy of the Archbishop of Canterbury. 'There was', recalls Brother Roger, 'a whole host of people, a hierarchy of churchmen, and the number of talks was considerable. For my part, I could not speak. How could I ever speak in front of all those people? Impossible!' He did not address the crowd assembled in the church, but on the evening of the inauguration he did overcome an ill-founded sense of his verbal limitations sufficiently to draw the attention of the groups of churchmen present away from the brick-work of the building to the message that lay beyond it. 'Consciously or not,' he suggested, 'those who come to Taizé are searching for something beyond themselves. When they ask for bread, how can we offer them stones to look at? When they have been in the Church of Reconcili-ation, it is better for them to remember the call to reconcili-ation and, with this as a basis, to prepare the daily bread of their lives, rather than to return home with only the memory of stones.'

'Within me', confides Brother Roger, 'there was no inner festival. I did not dare tell my brothers that I was not very happy but I sensed that they understood. There we had a building that was far too big, a building I had not wanted. Fortunately, on the following Monday, as I came out of the sacristy there was a great rainbow in the sky. It had been raining, and I said to myself: "There is God's answer. This church will not immobilize us. It's an ark. It will be filled."' His intuition was to be realized. For a while he admits to entering the new building as little as possible, but by Easter 1963 the space provided by the Church of Reconciliation was in urgent demand, and eight years after that it became necessary to knock down the rear wall and replace it with huge doors which could be raised to allow for a marquee extension. As far as accommodation for the growing crowd of young inter-national visitors was concerned, Brother Roger remained concerned that the community should not think on too large a scale. 'Hence the necessity to have tents, and as we never had money in hand we bought second-hand tents, old things that were vast but inoperative. When the wind blew they would tear apart, but it was enough to provide a minimum of welcome.'

It was not until some years later that Brother Roger became fully aware of a coincidence which he remains uncertain how to interpret. In 1947 the mother of a family had told him how, as she was walking along praying, she had come to the end of the village and had a vision of a high cross. She had insisted on pointing out the exact spot but, somewhat embarrassed by the story, Brother Roger had spoken of it to no one. When the time came to build the new church, Brother Roger wanted it to be close to the brothers' house. Several of his brothers, however, preferred it to be at a distance and that was what was done. Some time later Brother Roger realized that the building was sited on the very spot where years previously the woman had seen the great cross.

In his heart, one senses, Brother Roger still holds a special affection for the Romanesque church in the village and perhaps too for its tranquil seclusion. 'Initially,' he says, 'all this was so very far from our vision of things.' Yet it was, he recognizes, an indication that the parable of communion was not to be limited to one small corner of the world. It was a sign that was touching an ever increasing number of people: 'We had to accept that the way passed through mankind. That is the primary way.'

The same year in which the Church of Reconciliation was completed, 1962, was also to witness the conclusion of the war in Algeria, a war which had lasted eight years. In the course of a century considerable hatred had built up between the Arabs and the French in Algeria, and even amongst French people themselves the war had created deep divisions. For almost the entire duration of the fighting some of the brothers had lived in Algeria, in one of the first fraternities. They made their home in a hut built of planks and shared the living conditions of the occupants of a poor Arab neighbourhood. There were no other European residents. Indeed it was rare for a European to venture there even by day. The brothers were protected by the Arab population who recognized that they were men of peace. Nevertheless their lives were exposed to danger; at times when the war was at its height they would hear the whistle of passing bullets and a corner of their hut would retain the mark of a stray shot. The brothers stayed in Algeria for some time after the end of the war, so as to be present while the construction of the new Algeria was initiated. They remained until the creation of fraternities elsewhere called them to other places of human poverty and distress.

Other needs closer to the small village of Taizé were making themselves felt in a very concrete fashion. As early as 1951, as soon as there were twelve brothers, two of them had gone to live and work at Montceau-les-Mines in the poor mining area, thirty miles north of Taizé. The motivation was ever the same: the life of prayer impelled them to share their existence with those who were sorely tried. Three years later the brothers had been approached by a number of local farmers who were fearful about the future of their milk production. In an attempt to force down prices, the factory which had hitherto been responsible for collecting their milk was threatening to stop doing so. Under the supervision of a brother who had studied agriculture, the community's own farm was beginning to flourish, and on his advice it was decided that the solution to the problem lay in the formation of a milk co-operative for the region. The combined efforts of the local dairy farmers and the brothers were highly successful and soon the co-operative was collecting and processing milk from over a thousand producers. Then, in

1961, came Pope John XXIII's encyclical, *Mater at Magistra*, in which he spoke of socialization, calling in quite strong terms upon peasants and farmers throughout the world to co-operate with one another. The success of their farm, the fact that the cattle they had raised won prizes, had already begun to be a source of some unease to the brothers. In response to the papal encyclical, therefore, they decided with five farming families in the area to set up a total farming co-operative. In the Copex, as it was called, all land was pooled and all work done communally. 'There were some difficulties at first,' remembers Brother Roger with a smile. 'Our selected cattle had to adjust to living outside with the others – they had what you might call family problems.' Nevertheless the Copex worked well, so well in fact that it was used as a model for others and in 1964 the brothers, still concerned as to whether they should own any property at all, gave all the farmland they possessed to the Copex.

'When you establish the centre of your universe within yourself,' Brother Roger has written, 'you are plunged into egocentricity and your creative energies, your love, is dislocated.' The same principle, it may be suggested, might be applied to life in community. Taizé was being called upon increasingly to look outside itself, to live the parable of community in ever widening spheres of which possibly none was more important than that of the search for reconciliation in the broad arena of the universal Church. Furthermore, the universal Church is called upon to be the ferment of reconciliation in the entire human family. It was ever felt, but is now increasingly stressed, that the vision of reconciliation embraces not merely Christians but the whole of mankind. Whether recognized or not, Christ accompanies every human being. The communion which is the Church may have as its visible contours the body of Christ but at the same time

Above *Geneviève, Roger's youngest sister, with some of the twenty orphaned boys she took in at the end of the Second World War and looked after in a house in the village. This photograph was taken in May of 1954*

Below *Brother Roger and his adopted goddaughter from India, Marie Louise Sonaly, named after his grandmother*

*Church leaders are frequent visitors
to Taizé. Shown here are Michael Ramsey
when he was Archbishop of Canterbury
and Dr Eugene Carson Blake (then General
Secretary of the World Council of Churches)*

*The daily prayer at Taizé in the Church
of Reconciliation*

*Pope John Paul II receiving the brothers
during a European meeting of young people
in Rome*

*Prayer in St Paul's Cathedral during
the European meeting of young people
in London in 1981*

In Calcutta, during his time there in 1976

Mother Teresa talking with Brother Roger
whilst on a visit to Taizé

The village of Taizé

in the heart of God it is far more extensive than the human mind can conceive.

On 10 October 1962 the Second Vatican Council was opened in Rome. Among the observers at the opening ceremony stood two young guests of the newly created Secretariat for Christian Unity. Brother Roger and Brother Max were subsequently to be present at virtually every moment of every session from John XXIII's opening address to the Council's conclusion. 'I think,' recalls Brother Roger, 'I might have missed two morning sessions – once I was invited to visit a monastery near Rome and on another occasion I was the guest of an Italian bishop.' There had been those who had attempted to prevent them from coming to Rome, but the new mystical image of the Church as presented by John XXIII brought new hope and enthusiasm even in the face of opposition. 'At the Council, the Pope said we were going to refresh, to make the face of God more visible, make it more transparent, smooth away the wrinkles. He was a universal pastor with a vocation to actualize his ecumenical pastorate and to do so very simply for the benefit of the humble with whom Christ has identified himself. He himself was so transparent, like an open book.' The confidence the Bishop of Rome inspired in the Prior of Taizé did not go without response. 'Ah Taizé,' exclaimed John XXIII on greeting Brother Roger at an audience towards the end of his papacy, 'that little springtime!'

Sadly, the man who had been the initiator of the Council was not to see its conclusion. By 1963 it was clear to many that the Pope was very ill. Seeing his approaching death, Brother Roger sought a final audience with him, and it was a mark of the special rapport between the two men that Brother Roger was asked to be prepared to be called at any time. The Pope was not well enough for a date to be fixed in advance but Brother Roger would be summoned on 'a good day'. Three months before Pope John XXIII died Brother Roger and two other brothers were admitted for a last audience in the Pope's library. It had previously been a source of some amusement that people went to see the Pope armed with ten questions and never reached the third because he talked for so long in response to the first. On this occasion, however, there was only one question in the forefront of Brother Roger's mind, namely: could a way be found for the reconciliation of Christians to be achieved without anyone becoming a symbol of repudiation of their family of origin? Without, as another brother put it, re-enacting the story of Newman – not that Newman's suffering and action was not appreciated but it belonged to a different era, a different set of circumstances. The meeting was a long and an important one. 'One might have expected the response of a man who was a traditionalist, a conservative, from an Italian peasant background, but not at all. During that long audience God spoke. The Pope did not want to assume the role of a great spiritual teacher. In the gospel there are no spiritual teachers. He spoke very simply, giving me to understand that he realized that there was in us a certain unease. He did not impose a precise way. Instead he told me to continue the way we were. He did not want us to be too preoccupied, to ask ourselves too many questions. "You are in the Church," he told us, "for the church is ever-widening concentric circles." Precisely in what circle he saw us he did not specify, but the answer to our question as to how we should move forward without wounding those who had a common origin, how we should accomplish our vocation in the unique communion that is the Church, lay in that simple vision of a man of God.'

'On the evening of his death', Brother Roger continues, 'the Monday of Pentecost, June 1963, we went to church for evening prayer. It was eight o'clock or eight-thirty here when his death was announced, and we were at prayer. I told myself to thank God for his life, just to say one word, but the word would not come out. The ground opened beneath my feet that this immense confidence that had been granted to us at the very heart of the Church was no more. I retired to my room and remained there alone.'

Some time later, looking back on his last meeting with John XXIII, Brother Roger was to write of how he had seen the Pope weep because his intentions had been distorted. 'I realized', wrote Brother Roger, 'that his prophetic ministry had been refused and that an hour of ecumenism had been thereby lost.' John XXIII had not wanted attempts at unity to be turned into historical trials, nor to seek who was right and who was wrong. He had not hesitated to invite non-Catholics to the Second Vatican Council in defiance of many people's opinions, and he had suffered because non-Catholics had failed to offer any real response. A prophet had been rejected, ears had been blocked. 'Thenceforth,' wrote Brother Roger, 'ecumenism would sink into a way of parallelism, different denominations followed their separate ways, in a state of simple passive co-existence, and no more.'

The loss of the man who had been so faithful a confidant was deeply felt. 'Sometimes', Brother Roger has said, 'it is easier to accept one's own death than the death of another.' There is in him the conviction that he should still be able to communicate joy to others in circumstances that cause him great personal pain but he admits, with regret, that it is a conviction he is not always able to put into practice. The vacuum was to be further magnified by the death a short time later of Cardinal Gerlier. 'At the moment of his death I was asleep,' recalls Brother Roger. 'It was a Sunday morning, and suddenly a biblical text came into my sleep. I awoke and a little while later the telephone rang to tell me that the Cardinal had just died.

The text came from St Paul. I think it was, "Who now rejoice in my sufferings for you, and fill up that which is behind of the afflictions of Christ in my flesh for his body's sake, which is the Church" [Colossians 1.24]. Those two men who had shown us the way were no more.'

The vision of John XXIII, the Pope whom he loved and who returned his love, was to remain powerfully present to Brother Roger. In times of obscurity, he admits, he likes to call to mind the Pope's words, 'Be joyful, seek the best and let the sparrows chirp,' and faith in the prayer of one who is in eternity with God is a continued source of strength to him. In 1969 Brother Roger paid a visit to Sotto-el-Monte, John XXIII's home village, and members of the Roncalli family have come to Taizé on a number of occasions. It is with affection that Brother Roger recalls how the late Pope's brother was filled with spontaneous wonder and admiration at the sight of the tents and the simplicity of life of the young people on the hillside at Taizé, and one of his remarks in particular moved Brother Roger deeply. 'From here', commented Giuseppe Roncalli to his grandson who had accompanied him, 'will spring something that my brother started.'

It would seem that in Brother Roger's mind no one could quite replace John XXIII, by whose words the community live, although some years later he would refer to the Abbé Buisson in Culles-les-Roches as a man who in a small way had taken the place of John XXIII. The Abbé Buisson's 'confidence, his inner attitude, his understanding of existence,' explains Brother Roger, 'made it possible to discern that he was penetrating, beginning to see the invisible'. That vision was to be a source of inspiration to Taizé. Renewed hope came also with the election of Cardinal Montini as Paul VI. Towards the end of Pius XII's papacy and during that of John XXIII, Brother Roger had met Cardinal Montini on several occasions and had come to respect his advice. Having attended the funeral of John XXIII, Brother Roger was on board ship when he heard the news of the election of the successor to the See of Peter. 'I had to withdraw to my cabin. Montini was a man who was sensitive to everything, so intellectually gifted with an exceptional capacity for analysis and synthesis, so conscious of human injustice, but did he have what it would take to continue the peaceful, serenely joyful line of John XXIII?'

In a letter written by Brother Roger during a stay in Milan some years earlier he had already said of Montini,' If ever this man is made Pope, what a good Pope he will be.' 'And he was,' reflects Brother Roger with hindsight. 'We needed a man who would render the goodness of God transparent by everything that he was, and Paul VI was a profoundly good man, very close to the sanctity of Jesus Christ. He did not cut us off. Throughout his ministry he remained ever ready to listen.'

Almost immediately upon his election Paul VI announced his intention of continuing the Council. Brother Roger, Brother Max and three other brothers, based in the little flat they had found amongst some half-empty buildings in the centre of Rome, continued to attend the Council until its conclusion in 1965.

This small apartment was to become the setting for one of the fraternities. The role of the brothers in fraternity is 'to be signs of the presence of Christ and bearers of joy', an objective which in Rome at that time found its effective expression in hospitality offered to churchmen of a wide variety of confessions attending the Council. The gathering together of the brothers and their guests over a simple lunch or evening meal was for Brother Roger a form of agape, 'a foretaste of what we shall receive on the day visible unity comes about, in a single common Eucharist', for those who could not yet communicate at the same table. The meals often resounded with laughter. Brother Roger recalls with amusement briefing his brothers to cough should he say something inappropriate in the presence of certain guests and the resultant sudden bouts of coughing. Often the encounters would end with prayer in the small oratory created by the brothers in their flat, and with the birth of new friendships.

Strong links were forged with non-Catholics invited to the Council, with members of the Greek and Russian Orthodox Churches, and in particular with American Protestants who were keen that Taizé should send brothers to the United States, an invitation which was to open a new page in the subsequent history of the community. A number of links were also formed with South American bishops – with Cardinal Silva Henriquez of Chile, Dom Antonio Fragoso of Brazil, Bishop Manuel Larrain of Talca and Dom Helder Camara of Recife – a fact which may well have contributed to a special focusing on Latin America and its problems on the part of Taizé in the early sixties.

In a statement to the Paris press in 1963 Brother Roger had expressed his concern at the conflict between Christians in South America and at the poverty of its rapidly increasing population. In response to this challenge, Brother Roger's avowed intention was to join with the 'sons of that continent in their dedication'. Accordingly, as part of 'Operation Hope' Taizé organized an ecumenical collection of funds 'to help finance initiatives taken by Latin Americans themselves, with a view to restoring some hope in life to people who have lost all hope'. Latin American bishops had decided to relinquish land which had hitherto belonged to the Church. The money further enabled these bishops to help poverty-stricken peasants to start farming co-operatives on the donated land. The help was not, however, to be purely material. 'At the end of the Council,' recalls Brother Roger, 'Bishop Larrain came to me and asked me whether it would be possible to obtain copies of the New Testament in Spanish with the appropriate idiomatic peculiarities for Latin American countries, and to distribute them, asking the recipients to promise that they would meditate upon it with ten other people who were unable to read for themselves.' The community applied itself assiduously to the task. A commission of theologians worked on the translation and one million free copies in Spanish and 500,000 in Portuguese were distributed in packets of twenty all over South America. All the bishops were contacted and nearly everyone approached replied, providing addresses of appropriate recipients, a fact which Brother Roger saw as remarkable because he had been advised that in Latin America people were very reluctant to reply to letters. Also remarkable was the fact that so enormous a venture was embarked upon as an act of faith before any of the necessary funds were available. They were ultimately obtained as a result of collections launched by Brother Roger in every country in Europe.

Later, as a continuation of Operation Hope, Taizé was to provide a home for South Asian refugees from a camp in Thailand, to help victims of flooding in Bangladesh and of the drought in Sahel, to set up small schools in Haiti, and to send provisions to Poland after the *coup d'etat*.

Other friendships were formed elsewhere and among the most valued was that which developed with Athenagoras, Patriarch of Constantinople. Brother Roger first visited Constantinople at the Patriarch's invitation, for Athenagoras had suggested that he should create an Orthodox Taizé. To Brother Roger, however, the idea seemed inappropriate. In the light of the attempt to live a parable of community it would be more meaningful if the Patriarch were to send one or two monks to join the community at Taizé. The welcome Brother Roger received in Constantinople was embarrassing in its opulence, but he found Athenagoras to be a man in the same prophetic vein as John XXIII: 'We could have been in the early Church. He showed such confidence!' When Brother Roger told him that John XXIII could not do everything he wanted to, that there were those around him who blocked the texts he wrote, the Patriarch replied, 'If the Pope cannot do all that he would like to, I love him all the more.'

During that first meeting Athenagoras insisted upon Brother Roger accepting a present, an icon which the Prior of Taizé subsequently kept in his room. He also insisted that they went out together on a tour of the holy places. Seated on either side of the Patriarch, Brother Roger and Brother Max were taken in an imposing car to all the local sites of Christian martyrdom, and at each spot the Patriarch paused to pray. At the end of the tour he did not want the brothers to leave. Never to part, as Athenagoras wished, would have been an impossible proposition for Brother Roger. They were, however, to meet again on a number of subsequent occasions – in Rome, upon Mount Athos and in Constantinople – and the Patriarch did in fact send an Orthodox monk to live for a while at Taizé. During Brother Roger's later visit to Constantinople in 1970 the Patriarch, in a significant and heartfelt gesture towards union, twice declared that for him Brother Roger was a priest, that he could make his confession to the Prior of Taizé and receive from him the body and blood of Christ. At the moment of their parting Patriarch Athenagoras raised his hands as if elevating a chalice. 'The cup and the breaking of bread,' were his last words to Brother Roger. 'Remember that is the only way.'

Sadly, both in the Catholic Church and elsewhere, the brothers' attempts to forge links proved at times less obviously fruitful. There were many in Protestant circles who were sympathetic to the search for means of reconciliation and indeed to the idea of a community. Many Protestant pastors came to the hill of Taizé; some to spend days in silent retreat, others to take part with their wives in meetings for married couples led by the brothers. Numerous German, Swiss and Dutch pastors also brought their parish groups to Taizé for weekends of prayer and reflection. For some, however, the question dating back to the sixteenth century as to whether life-long commitment to celibacy did not in fact represent a limitation of the freedom of the Holy Spirit, remained a burning one. It was an issue which the brothers of Taizé viewed rather in the light of an effective demonstration of the liberty of the Holy Spirit. Was not the Spirit alive enough to call someone to lifelong commitment? Nevertheless this question remained a primary reason why there were those who expressed their concern that Taizé should not be taken as representative of Protestantism as a whole. The fact that the brothers were equally concerned that they should not be labelled a specifically Protestant community appears not to have allayed the fears of some. There remained those who misunderstood the brothers' intentions and who felt that Taizé had no right to set itself up as a form of ecumenical arbitrator.

Among Brother Roger's memories of the World Council of Churches in Geneva there is nonetheless the recollection of 'so many transparent faces, visible reflections of the sanctity of Christ'. With the World Council of Churches very special relations were established when in 1966 the American Eugene Carson Blake was made its new leader. 'Eugene Carson Blake was', recalls Brother Roger, 'a man of the Holy Scriptures, a man who understood.' As soon as he had been nominated and before taking up his appointment he expressed a wish to visit Taizé, and when he did meet Brother Roger he asked him to pass on a message of sympathy and understanding to the Pope. 'He asked me to tell Paul VI that he had seen him on his balcony at Castelgandolfo and to say how much confidence and sympathy he felt, how much he loved his ministry.' Carson Blake was an American pastor and perhaps his great readiness to look forward rather than back stemmed from his origins in a country where there are fewer references to history.

The American General Secretary visited Taizé on numerous occasions and was quick to invite one of the brothers to attend the World Council of Churches in Geneva with a view to stimulating the life of prayer at the Council. In 1968 he invited Brother Roger to address the World Council Assembly in Uppsala and in the following year he suggested that the community collaborate in the work of SODEPAX, the joint commission for justice and peace of the Vatican and the World Council of Churches. So it was that, at Carson Blake's instigation, one of the brothers came to spend several years cementing the relationship between Rome, Geneva and Taizé. Sadly, this brother later died suddenly and prematurely, but after his death it became apparent in many quarters how much his work had been appreciated. Prior to a gathering of young people at Taizé during Easter 1972 Carson Blake spoke of his appreciation of the community's efforts in a way that touched the brothers deeply:

In attending the meeting of young people that you are preparing for Easter [he declared], I shall be undertaking my fourth journey to Taizé in the space of one year. I appreciate your community's search to emerge from the current ecumenical impasses, a search which you are undertaking with tens of thousands of young people from all over the world, and your efforts to take part in the quest for greater justice among men.

I firmly believe that regular personal contacts favour ecumenical exchanges. That is why I have been happy that a brother from Taizé, attached for some years on a full-time basis to SODEPAX has made a permanent exchange possible between the community and the ecumenical centre at Geneva.

Carson Blake's term of office as a whole was to bring great joy to the Taizé community. On one occasion he even suggested that at Taizé the Eucharist should be celebrated at two altars according to two confessions. 'If all go to the Catholic Eucharist,' he said, 'we shall rejoice in the fact.' The brothers were unable to take up his suggestion but the anecdote is recalled with warmth as an indication of his generosity of spirit. There were, however, too many barriers in the American pastor's way. Some time before he was officially due to retire from his position he announced in Addis Ababa that he was resigning. The ecumenical desert which had followed the death of John XXIII, Brother Roger told him, would become even greater without him. Indeed, in the period following the Second Vatican Council a certain atmosphere of disillusionment had set in, a feeling prevailed that much of the promise offered by the ecumenical movement had remained unfulfilled, and there were many who suffered in consequence.

After his initial misunderstanding, Pastor Marc Boegner, president of the Federation of Protestant Churches of France had become a regular visitor and friend to Taizé. His wife too 'understood everything from within'. When they died, copies of the Taizé office were placed in their coffins for they had both used them daily. Prior to her father's death Boegner's daughter asked Brother Roger to visit him in Paris. 'He had a question to ask me and the question was this: "Should we now, after the Vatican

Council, say that the brackets should be closed on Protestantism?" All that I said to him was, "Of course you should say so, because all the reforms sought after in the sixteenth century have been achieved and more!" To myself I thought that such a statement would not carry a great deal of weight, because structures, history, everything that was so strongly, heavily present could not be so easily modified, but as a spiritual testament it would have its value. Afterwards I learned that Boegner had asked the same question of someone else and that that person had restrained him altogether. Perhaps it was to the good. There would have been suffering from the polemics and the contradictions that followed. There is always the question in life as to whether what is right for one, holds good when there are several. How will those you love bear up? Sometimes there is a need for restraint.'

The eve of the Second Vatican Council had given birth to the hope of a prompt reconciliation between the non-Catholic Churches and the Church of Rome. 'In the years that followed,' Brother Roger has written, 'the spirit of unity favoured new understandings and friendships. Remarkable theological documents were compiled. But with time it became apparent that that reconciliation was as if projected into a more or less distant future.' Many ecumenical bodies had been created, but denominations embarked upon parallel courses and a kind of passive coexistence was established between them. It was as if ecumenism had in some way reached a ceiling.

'We had hoped for reconciliation between the Churches themselves. It had to be accepted that that path was impracticable but,' assures Brother Roger, 'God never condemns anyone to immobility. He never closes paths. He is always opening new ones even if at times they are narrow. God had already prepared for us another way.'

5

CREATING TOGETHER

On the hillside of Taizé the discussion groups on the subject of ecumenism had begun to reflect a certain decline in interest, yet people continued to come there in increasing numbers, predominantly young people but adults too. The community did not seek this afflux, nor did it try to increase it. Indeed, it did not altogether understand what was happening. The brothers themselves were increasing in number and with the addition of members from Holland, Germany, the United States and Britain the community was becoming ever more international. Confronted by the arrival of so many young people, the brothers simply reacted as they felt any religious community would; they made the pilgrims welcome. Many of them, it was recognized, had faith in God but experienced a growing indifference to the problems of the Church. The community sought to provide a response. 'In all of us there is to a greater or lesser degree a pastoral gift,' suggests Brother Roger, 'and the young people activate in us, awake in us that gift and develop it.' It was as part of this response that Brother Roger wrote *Unanimity in Pluralism* (1966), a book in which he endeavoured to offer a more positive vision of the pluralism which, to some at least, represented a source of concern in the years following the Second Vatican Council. That pluralism was something, he insisted, not to be feared but rather to be discussed constructively. One principle that had emerged from the Council had touched a chord of recognition in him, namely that there was in the Christian faith a 'hierarchy of truths'. Not all elements of faith were of equal importance; some were essential while others were secondary. In this principle lay the key to a continuing hope of reconciliation, for what was needed was a central pillar which was unanimity, around which pluralism could exist. Taking the pain that many were suffering at the time, he did not attempt to contradict or deny its existence but recentred it, asserting the value of the transfiguration. Christ does not destroy or reject but takes man as he is and transforms even the worst in him.

Unanimity in Pluralism was not the first book that Brother Roger had written and published since setting down *The Rule of Taizé*. It was the third of three books which he now considers could have been composed as a single work and one of a number of books, the titles of which provide a concrete reflection of a line of progression. Brother Roger himself admits to preferring to develop his ideas through dialogue rather than the written word. Finding, to his own surprise, new inspiration and a surge of enthusiasm in answer to a complex question put directly to him, he adds as an appendage to his answer of the moment: 'That is how I like to respond – when I am carried away.' A book, once completed, is in a sense immediately outdated, in need of modification, and so it is that Brother Roger prefers not to reread his own writings. The need constantly to rewrite and to change things is doubtless fundamental to his character for he admits to never reading a novel without wanting to rewrite it and he finds his relaxation by rearranging furniture. Yet there is in him also a reluctance to be rushed. At his specific request one early book, published somewhat hurriedly because of the need for finances, was never reprinted.

After the writing of *The Rule* there followed a long interval during which no books were published. In the first version of *The Rule of Taizé* there is an allusion to the fact that what was not set down there would be stipulated in what is known in monastic tradition as the 'customary law'. Brother Roger made several attempts to write this last but never actually completed it. Eventually, all reference to it was dropped, because he found it an impossible contradiction to set down in writing and thus on permanent record those elements of the common life that were likely to be constantly modified. Consequently Taizé has no customary law, no constitution. Having also first deliberately abandoned his vision of authorship, Brother Roger appears subsequently to have doubted his ability to write at all. He did, however, compile a number of articles and, despite a feeling of being ill-equipped to speak in public, he talked a little; it was this material which was ultimately reworked to form the basis of a book entitled *Living Today for God* (1959). 'Those words', recalls one of the brothers, 'exerted a strong influence at that time. The message was not new. It was contained in the Sermon on the Mount: sufficient unto the day is the evil thereof, why therefore worry about tomorrow? But it was perhaps very existential; it touched the very existence of man.' In relation to the path of reconciliation it implied that the way should not be allowed to be impeded by the past nor caught up in the future but lived in the present. As far as the community was concerned, it was already a foreshadowing of a more recent theme at Taizé, that of confidence, and suggested that the brothers should not be unduly committed to long-term projects or elaborate programmes. Characteristically, Brother Roger was subsequently to write in his journal that the title should really have been 'Living the Moment for God'. However, it remained unaltered for fear of misunderstanding. It was, after all, recognized that a certain continuity is also needed in life. The community at Taizé does live the Today. It has no archives, and much of the documentation of the past has been destroyed in order to prevent the wrong kind of nostalgia and to foster a spirit of receptivity, forgiveness and reconciliation. 'Having put your hand to the plough,' claims Brother Roger, 'the important thing is not to look backwards but to go forwards.' Only by these means can the hope of a constant springtime in the community's existence be nurtured. There are a few fixed elements in that existence. Important dates for the future are set, but apart from these there is a great deal of flexibility and freedom in a way that is entirely consistent with a Rule that stipulates very little definite shape even for the day. For Brother Roger it is a way of life to which he is naturally suited. 'He has', concedes one of the brothers with evident affection, 'a great deal of human experience, intuition, maturity, but there is too something of the child about him. Everything is very immediate. He does not have much notion of time.'

Published in 1965, *The Dynamic of the Provisional* was a more explicit expansion of the fundamental idea expressed in *Living Today for God*. For Brother Roger it was a means of conveying the idea that energy arises out of the avoidance of too much rigidity. It was written at a time when the Second Vatican Council was in the process of answering many questions on the subject of reform. Underlining the movement of modern man away from static traditions in the direction of 'continuous creativity', Brother Roger raised the question as to whether the Reformation itself was not in reality provisional. Sadly, the title was much misunderstood. To some it smacked of anti-establishment ideology and others chose deliberately to misuse it in that sense.

Only months after the conclusion of the Vatican Council Brother Roger, together with Brother Max, produced a small book entitled *The Living Word at the Council*, which included not only an insight into what a day at the Council entailed but also a French translation of the dogmatic constitution *Dei Verbum* on revelation and a point-by-point commentary on it. 'The Spirit blows where it wills,' wrote the Jesuit, Henri de Lubac, in his preface to the work:

> At the very time when some among us, as if suddenly struck by blindness, seem no longer to perceive the beauty or the benefit to the world, of the evangelic words that are the source and the norm of the religious life in the Church, on the plateau of Taizé, once a nearby dependency of ancient Cluny, a swarm of young men from all the horizons of the Protestant Reformation have gathered to lead that life together, a life they are rediscovering in all its freshness.

Furthermore, de Lubac went on to say, it was precisely at an hour when some seemed on the point of vacillating in their attachment to the tradition of the Church, which transmits in its living actuality, the word of God, that the two brothers had provided a book which would strengthen that attachment.

From the very briefest consideration of some of Brother Roger's writings it becomes strikingly apparent that they are the product of a profound awareness and understanding of the concerns and preoccupations of the many for whom Taizé provides a listening ear. 1968, for example, was a year of violent eruptions; the shootings in the Square of Three Cultures in Mexico, the Russian invasion of Czechoslovakia, and the student demonstrations and the month-long general strike in France. In the United States too, it was a year of heated demonstrations, and at Taizé inevitably the issue of violence had become a central one. This was also, however, the period that witnessed the expansion of the peace movement. So it was that Brother Roger published a book entitled *Violent for Peace*, which accepted the existence of inner violence in all men but which called once more for its transfiguration. Mankind, he asserts, cannot be non-violent for to be so would be a denial of its humanity. It is a question, therefore, of how that inner violence can be used, and the solution proposed is that we should let it become the violence of those who live the Beatitudes, the violence of the peace makers. There is creativity, he asserts, in the very tension that exists between two apparently opposite poles of this kind.

The year 1968 was also a time when the questions asked by visitors to Taizé began to reflect the fact that people were more interested in how they should actually live their lives than in ideas alone. They had begun to ask the Taizé community innumerable personal questions about their life together, and for this reason in *Violent for Peace* Brother Roger began to publish brief extracts from his diary. The inclusion of these passages was a prompt and sensitive response to the recognition of a need to understand via the person. It was also a form of communication which suited Brother Roger well, for he found himself ever more reluctant to elaborate on a whole thought in a carefully structured manner. The diary form which he was to use increasingly from then onwards would allow him to suggest an idea, then return to it next day or several days later to correct, modify or expand the subject if he felt that he had dealt with it inadequately. It would also, he thought, enable him to appease the reader if he had expressed something too tactlessly and to juxtapose a wide variety of themes. This is also, it should be added, how he likes to speak. In recent years his brothers have persuaded him to talk into a microphone when he addresses them at meals, partly because his voice is not strong, and partly no doubt because they would like what he says placed at least on private record; they will vouch for the fact that he will frequently return to a particular idea on a number of different occasions to offer a new dimension to it on the strength of further reflection or the reactions of others to what he has previously said.

Not insignificantly, some of the brothers assist in the task of choosing which of Brother Roger's diary entries should or should not be published, in a way which satisfies the desire to create not in isolation but together, a principle which governs every aspect of their common life and which manifestly extends to embrace the needs and gifts of those outside the community also. It was perhaps this readiness to listen, to absorb and to amend in response to differing viewpoints which brought young people to Taizé in their thousands at a time when society seemed to offer few other places where older people were prepared to seek to understand, and possibly even to attempt to change existing structures as a consequence of what they heard. 'In the world in general 1969 to 1970 were very sad years,' recounts one of the brothers. 'There was trouble in Czechoslovakia. There was a crisis in society. There was also an incipient crisis in the Church caused by among other factors the contradictory hopes placed in the Vatican Council. A movement of priests and religious away from the Church had begun. Journalists everywhere were focusing on bad news, and so at Taizé the question arose as to what could be announced by way of glad tidings.' The question had also arisen as to how a certain continuity could be established between the weeks spent at Taizé and the visitors' daily lives. By this time it had become the general practice for visitors to come to Taizé for a week during which they could choose to spend their time in silence, apart from daily talks with a brother who would accompany them in their retreat, in the practical work inevitably involved in accommodating large numbers of guests, or in discussion groups in which people of many nations, speaking a wide variety of languages, were mixed together and themes were raised, such as that of how the search for reconciliation could be furthered. How then could people remain in touch with each other after their stay at Taizé and together continue that quest without thereby creating the structures of a movement? Thus, twenty years later and on a much larger scale, Taizé was to encounter once more the problem that the Grande Communauté had posed during the Community's infancy; to be joined in a common search was one thing, but to form a group with its own structure, closed in upon itself, was quite another. Taizé has never wanted a movement to be linked to the community. It was resolved that visitors would return to their respective countries and homes with certain questions, for which each person would seek an answer from his or her particular situation. For what, for example, were they really searching? What would enable Christ's Church to free itself from its divisions? What joyful news did young people have to offer to the people of God? In February 1969 it had been noted that forty-two nations were represented on the hill, despite the fact that this was considered a quiet period of the year. 'We are', reflected

Brother Roger, 'like a council of youth.' 'For months past,' he later wrote in his journal, 'one thing has been preoccupying me: with the present discord in the Church, what act could give peace to those who are shaken, and strength to those who are committed? I sense that such an act should be a gathering of an exacting nature, regularly repeated for the years to come over a certain period of time, building and searching together. And with that, again and again the same thought dominates: this demanding gathering is going to be a council of youth.' In Latin, Germanic and Slavic languages there are two possible words for 'council'. The one deliberately chosen was the expression specifically used to denote church assemblies such as the former ecumenical councils, the Second Vatican Council or important local church gatherings. The idea of a council of youth clearly evoked the fact that this was to be a church quest, rooted in the celebration of prayer and not a forum of abstract ideas. The word also suggested an event that would be provisional, that would last for a certain period but have a conclusion. Once more the concern that there should be no structured movement, no 'Taizé Communion', found its expression. Several months before announcing the Council of Youth, Brother Roger spoke to Paul VI about the project to meet with an encouraging response. 'Get it on the rails,' was Paul VI's reply.

The announcement of the Council of Youth was made on Easter Day 1970 and it was eventually opened four years later. It was entirely appropriate that the most important moments in the course of its preparation should take place at Easter, for the prayer and expression of faith at Taizé has always been centred on the resurrection, on the paschal mystery. Even the white habit of the community is related to the significance it gives to Easter, for white is the colour of resurrection and of joy. Prior to the Vatican Council, it is perhaps true to suggest, there was more emphasis amongst Christians in general upon Good Friday and suffering. For the community of Taizé, however, the accent has always been on the joy of the resurrection, and the paschal mystery is seen as paramount in the 'hierarchy of truths'. It was as natural, therefore, that from 1970 onwards annual gatherings should be held on the feast of the resurrection as it was that the prayer at Taizé should eventually revolve round the celebration of a weekly Easter. Because too, of the number of young Latin American bishops present at Taizé at the time, the celebration of the *Pascua juvenil* spread like wildfire through Latin American parishes and today is widespread. The fundamental idea of placing the emphasis with young people on the Easter festival has been introduced to Latin America only within the last twenty years and had its origins at Taizé.

The preparations that preceded the opening of the Council of Youth in 1974 and the subsequent celebrations in Latin America, North America, Asia and Africa have been well documented in *The Story of Taizé* by J. L. G. Balado and *Taizé: Brother Roger and his Community* by Rex Brico. It is enough here to look at what those years meant and evoked in more subjective terms for Brother Roger and the community. The need for glad tidings called forth not only the announcement of the Council of Youth but also *Festival Without End* (1971), a book the object of which was to encourage people not to lose heart but to live a festival in the joy offered by one who in the Sermon on the Mount seven times announced the happiness available to mankind. The title was a jubilant echo of the proclamation of St Athanasius that the risen Christ makes of the life of man a continuous festival. Our life as Christians, explains Brother Roger, consists of living continually the paschal mystery, of successive small deaths followed by the beginnings of resurrection. The origins of festival lie in the constructive use of the good and the less good in mankind. Festival, he also says, is like a small field which we cultivate within ourselves, a sports ground where freedom and spontaneity are exercised. Its boundaries are formed by the obligation not to violate the conscience or freedom of another. Juxtaposed with the spiritual search the concern for human justice thus makes itself implicitly felt. It finds its more explicit expression in a note which Brother Roger jotted down even before he came to Taizé: 'The stronger the urge for communion or the more one wishes to progress in a spiritual life of communion with God, the more essential it is to confront that life with everyday realities and to clasp it to the heart of human distress.' How can the Christian who is called to love fail to act when confronted by man as victim of his fellow man?

'The crisis continued,' recounts one of the brothers, 'and in a sense became even more complex. The young people coming to Taizé from Italy, Spain and France, for example, were increasingly politically minded. It was not necessarily a bad thing, because their politicization stemmed from an ardent desire for justice. They were prepared to struggle for human justice, but for some the mere word "Church" provoked negative reactions. Yet many of them wanted to pray, and to search for God.' Was there a contradiction between their readiness to struggle and their desire to pray? Was it a question of struggle or contemplation? Again in 1973 Brother Roger attempted to offer the beginnings of an answer in the form of a book entitled *Struggle and Contemplation* dedicated to Hamani Diori, the Muslim President of Niger, in which he stressed that there was no necessity to choose between the two. Both elements are born of love and the gospel tells us that it is impossible to love God without loving our brother also. The root of his suggested solution was not new, but like all the insights he so tentatively offers, it stemmed from personal experience and it was crucially important both for those who were passionately in favour of struggle and for those who were equally ardently opposed to it.

On the occasion of the opening of the Council of Youth in 1974 representatives of the Pope, the Patriarch of Constantinople, the Archbishop of Canterbury and of the different Protestant Churches were all present at Taizé. The opening enabled 40,000 young people from every continent to gather for several days on the hill and share their thirst for human justice, for reconciliation between Christians and indeed between all men. 'But', explains a brother, 'the call for reconciliation contained in their 'First Letter to the People of God', which was published at that time, was formulated in a tone that was perhaps a little too abrupt. In Western society the crisis was mounting. Consequently the crisis in the Church was also becoming more acute. Within each Church new divisions had appeared, adding to the old denominational divisions. Finding a path of reconciliation was becoming more and more complicated. It would take a whole process of maturation. That is why to this day the Council of Youth has not had a reunion since its opening.' Brother Roger was later to comment that the Council of Youth had been provisionally placed in abeyance, and that it would perhaps re-emerge after years of maturation. The community's course with the young people who would come to Taizé in growing numbers during the years that followed was therefore to take another form, to centre itself more specifically on the search for the sources of faith.

After the opening of the Council of Youth, there followed a period when turbulence subsided. The life of the Church entered into something of a morass and there was a prevailing feeling that nothing had come of all the unrest. Perhaps society could not be changed in the way that some had thought. Very little was happening. Was it possible, therefore, to expect something unhoped for? *A Life We Never Dared Hope For* (1976) was the result of this question, a response which was to be further developed in 1979 in *The Wonder of a Love*. St John tells us, 'In this is love, that God loved us first,' and in that assurance lies the foundation for the theme of confidence, the invitation to surrender oneself body and soul in the knowledge of God's unfailing love.

In the interim, profoundly moved by a period spent in the southern hemisphere amongst the poorest of the poor and again recognizing the preoccupations of the young people on the hill of Taizé, Brother Roger wrote of what he saw as the deserts of this world, the material and spiritual deserts, deserts of need and deserts of doubt and discouragement. Inspired perhaps by the joy and zest for life that welled up in the poor whose plight, rationally, is intolerably hard, he offers in *And Your Deserts Shall Flower* (1982) the assurance that in the desert of the heart unfailing resources well up, an inner life, an inner light. It is upon these same inner resources, one senses, that he himself, in his unflagging attempt to rise to each need identified, has become increasingly dependent. His initial intuition concerning a council of youth included the recognition of the magnitude of the demands that such a gathering would make upon the energy of the community. 'As far as we are concerned,' he wrote in his journal, 'there is no comparison between the effort needed and our possibilities.' 'Can you imagine,' he asks, 'what it takes simply to ensure that each one of the great wave of young people is personally welcomed?'

There was a time when the community considered moving elsewhere: it seemed the afflux of young people was becoming too heavy a load. 'One of my brothers said to me, "We must not remain here. We must go to a desert elsewhere. We cannot go on like this. Our vocation has been disfigured." Many brothers seemed to be of the same mind. For weeks we talked about it. We gathered together friends from the area who knew what was happening, but we came to the conclusion that we had no material means to make such a move possible. In any case we could not go anywhere except in France. To go far away was an attractive proposition but we knew that it would not be so simple today to insert the heart of a community in the world of the poor, in the Third World. Where could we find the deserts in this part of the world, perhaps up in the mountains but everyone agreed unanimously that we would be followed.' Furthermore, Brother Roger recognized that to turn his back on that following would be to abandon those young people in whom he has identified 'a thirst for communion' and to avert his eyes while they abandoned the Church. Many who came to Taizé were giving the Church a last chance. 'Were it not for this abandonment of the Church,' he admits, 'perhaps our life might have been different.'

In 1970 a group of young Italians sent a letter to churchmen in their country giving expression to their own thoughts, which were in conflict with those of their bishops, using the name of Brother Roger. They had photocopied his signature at the end of the letter. One of the recipients of the letter, who knew Brother Roger well, appealed to him to put an article in the press to rectify the situation. For Brother Roger, however, such an act was impossible. He could not, he said, disavow young people, even though they had acted in a manner of which he disapproved. All he could do would be to speak to them personally. With hindsight he does not know whether he was right in his decision because at that time the confidence of certain older people had been shaken. They had difficulty in understanding what was happening amongst the younger generation, although some years later the situation was to be eased by the fact that an increasing number of adults came to Taizé for international gatherings.

Brother Roger's sympathy for the young is deep-rooted. In his own youth he admits to having quite frequently encountered indifference when, for example, he wanted to object to the prevailing acceptance on the part of Christians of their multiple divisions. For this reason he wanted contemporary young people to find a more ready ear. He loves the fact that the young of today do not foster the spirit of caste. Not surprisingly too, the present generation of young people holds an attraction for him 'because they do not wear masks'. His own background is steeped in concealed emotions. The appeal of a generation where restraint and the maintenance of emotional distance is no longer called for to the same degree is not difficult to understand. Thus it was not Brother Roger's confidence in young people that was placed in jeopardy – for he has said repeatedly that he would go to the ends of the earth to proclaim his confidence in youth – but rather the confidence of some members of the older generation who feared that the young were exerting too much influence on him and on the community. This lack of understanding was to render Brother Roger ever more attentive to the rift that existed between the generations in the West and induced him, for example, in his 'Letter to all Generations' to call upon the young to try and find ways of bridging the gap.

It was during these years that the Prior of Taizé felt that the community had established firm enough roots to be in a position to envisage fraternities further afield, notably on the other side of the Atlantic. Leading members of the American Protestant Churches whom he had met in Rome during the Vatican Council had even suggested to him that he create a Taizé 'foundation' in the United States by buying a house where brothers sent from Taizé would live for their entire life and so in a sense intitiate another Taizé. The suggestion was not adopted because the brothers wished to remain a single small family and not to be split in two, but a provisional fraternity of a few brothers was established in the United States. Over the years its location has been altered several times and now the presence of Taizé in America takes two complementary forms: a number of brothers have installed themselves in a poor district in New York where the majority of residents are Puerto-Ricans, and from time to time brothers also lead a pilgrimage of reconciliation across the United States and Canada which means that several times a year they take part in meetings of young people in different parts of the two countries. Shortly after setting up a fraternity in North America the community turned its attention to Latin America, and some of the brothers set out for Brazil. After some twenty years they are still there today. First they lived for six years in Recife, the city of Dom Helder Camara with whom Brother Roger formed a friendship during the Council, then six further years were spent in a very poor part of Vitoria, before the brothers turned north-east to Alagoinhas. There they installed themselves in an outlying district of the city, sharing the existence of a population with a black majority. There too they provided a welcome for young people who came from all over Brazil for days of prayer and reflection.

For the brothers themselves 1969 had also incorporated a significant step forward in terms of the actual realization of a parable of communion. From its very earliest days the community had sustained a vision of the Church and of the Eucharist similar to that of the Roman Catholic and Orthodox Churches. It had not as yet, however, been led

110

to express itself in a very precise way with regard to the Bishop of Rome and his ministry as a universal pastor. The question was to become more pressing. By 1969 the community already counted amongst its members brothers from the Reformed, Anglican and Lutheran traditions, and there had been a number of attempts made to involve members of the Catholic faith in the parable of communion. It was significant, for example, that Charles de Foucauld's order of the Little Brothers of Jesus, born at approximately the same time as the Taizé community, had wanted in 1949 to send their brothers to live their postulancy at Taizé. The time had not yet been right, however, and they had not received permission from the Catholic authorities. Later, Benedictine and Franciscan monks had lived for a while in close proximity to the community. In the interim years a number of young individuals who were Catholics had also wanted to join the community. However, prior to 1969 their entry would have meant their separating themselves from the Catholic Church, and Taizé could never have tolerated the idea that a single Roman Catholic had ceased to belong to the Catholic Church because of Taizé. On the contrary, the brothers have frequently helped Catholics going through periods of crisis to rediscover their Catholic roots. Numerous priests on the point of leaving the ministry have been inspired by Taizé to remain faithful to their first commitment.

As far as the brothers were concerned, seeking as always to avoid developing as a purely Protestant community which would give further emphasis to the separate existence of the Churches of the Reformation, Brother Roger sought a solution with the advice of several bishops who were experts on Canon Law. Canon Law, he was warned, would present the community with insuperable obstacles. It was far too precise. An alternative method of approach existed in the form of common law. The process was to prove long and complex but would eventually bear fruit. At Easter 1969 a young doctor from Belgium became the first Catholic brother, with the approval of Cardinal Marty, Archbishop of Paris, and at the brothers' annual council a text was drawn up which was to make clear the community's position for the benefit of those who in the future might consider entering it. Thenceforth each non-Catholic brother must know that the community anticipated communion with Peter, with the Bishop of Rome:

> The mere presence of Catholic brothers among us stimulates us to live more and more in anticipation of unity, by being in communion with that minister who is the servant of the servants of God. No one is thereby asking us to disavow our Churches. They have communicated faith to us. But we seek to reconcile in our lives the Churches from which we originate and the Catholic Church, separated by a divorce.

'The Catholic soul of my grandmother,' Brother Roger reflects, 'in some way made this development possible, by her life and what she was.' That same spirit was to induce Brother Roger to speak out on the subject of the papal ministry, an issue which he always recognize to be ever delicate. 'We are contemporaries of John XXIII, that great witness of Christ,' Brother Roger told bishops of the Episcopal Church in New York in 1971. 'Is it now still possible for us to envisage the unity of the Church without so much as touching on the question of the Bishop of Rome? And yet there is still a conspiracy of silence around his ministry of unity, even among certain Catholics. Every local community needs a pastor, to gather together the flock always inclined to fragment and to scatter. Can we really hope to see the Church gather in unity unless it has a similar pastor for its universality? Surely his vocation is to be at the very heart of the Church's life, not at the top of a pyramid, or acting as a kind of head.'

In 1975 Brother Roger, in a letter which he was personally to take to Paul VI, outlined two requests to the Bishop of Rome: the first being that, as universal pastor, he should be attentive to justice among men and in the Church and so lead not only the Catholic Church but also the non-Catholic Churches towards a greater simplicity of means; secondly, he intimated that it fell to the Bishop of Rome to do everything possible to effect reconciliation between Christians without asking non-Catholics to deny their family origins. Would the Bishop of Rome not, therefore, open the Eucharist to all those baptized who believed in the real presence of the body and blood of Christ and who passionately seek unity of faith?

The entry of Catholic brothers into the community had highlighted this latter issue, which was always one of central concern at Taizé. In *The Dynamic of the Provisional* Brother Roger had predicted that the tide of ecumenism would fall away if the day did not soon come when all those who believed in the same way in the real presence of Christ could gather round the same table. It was a statement which touched a chord of recognition in many readers, not least of them Cardinal Bea in Rome who was struck by the fact that Brother Roger had not called for the unconditional opening of the Catholic Mass to everyone but to those who 'had confidence in the Catholic faith'. On this basis the Cardinal, who was responsible for ecumenism in Rome, felt that the Catholic Mass could be made open to Taizé and he offered to put a suggestion to that effect to Paul VI; 'You have a Eucharistic faith that is so Catholic', the Cardinal commented. At the time Brother Roger felt that if such a concession were made exclusively for Taizé it would create a source of polemic. Anxious to avoid any further contention associated with the name of Taizé, he suggested that such a proposal would only be acceptable if it was made applicable in other places also. In any case, he felt certain that ultimately a more general movement would be made in that direction. The Cardinal understood Brother Roger's response but the question arose as to whom else the same principle could be applied – and it remained unanswered. It is a decision which Brother Roger now regrets for, although with the consent of the local bishop and the bishops in whose dioceses the fraternities are located, a working arrangement has been found for the community, an opportunity for a door to be opened by the Pope himself was lost. The ecumenical movement was not in fact to take the course Brother Roger had anticipated.

While in the Church as a whole an impasse appeared to have been reached, in the Church of Reconciliation the brothers endeavoured to cater to all viewpoints. Catholic and non-Catholic priests and pastors celebrated Mass and the Lord's Supper respectively and the sacraments from the Catholic Mass were subsequently reserved. At the entrance to the Church of Reconciliation a text now hangs in six languages:

> The Catholic Eucharist is reserved and venerated next to the icon of the Virgin Mary. It is from this reserve that Communion is distributed each day.
>
> Receiving Communion daily (so called frequent Communion) is not customary in Protestantism. Protestants can receive the Lord's Supper at the entrance of the chapel to the right of the cross.

It is not a solution which the community regards as ideal: 'In the same way that we do not have a pastoral method for young people and that we do not even want there to be a spirituality of Taizé, we do not have a method with regard to ecumenism either. We do not profess to have found any solutions.' Brother Roger himself celebrated increasingly rarely for some considerable time and then ceased to do so altogether, preferring to be a brother and no more: 'My brothers understood the impossibility of my celebrating the Lord's Supper. I could not be anything other than a brother. My brothers smiled when I told them what I intended,' Brother Roger confided. 'They know me so well.' The need for a priest on the hill throughout the year would thenceforth be met by the diocesan priest in charge of the parishes around Taizé who also lived in the community.

It would be both inappropriate and inaccurate to exaggerate the role of the popes in the life and development of Taizé; the community is at pains to stress that throughout its history friendship and support has come from Catholics and non-Catholics alike. Yet it must remain true that the fact that from 1971 onwards there would be a permanent representative of the Prior of Taizé to the Holy See and that Paul VI consistently maintained his trust in the community is something which, like the confidence shown in many other quarters, the brothers value. Every year there were meetings between Brother Roger and the Pope, and it is an indication of the personal rapport between the two men that when Paul VI, the first Pope in centuries to travel outside Italy, flew to Bogota for the Eucharistic Congress and the opening of the Assembly of Bishops, he invited Brother Roger to join him for the flight. Paul VI liked to conduct his audiences on the basis of notes. Brother Roger would, therefore, send him a paper two or three days in advance outlining the issues he wished to raise. The Pope would study them carefully before speaking, and sought consistently to understand. Paul VI remained completely positive about the Council of

Youth, despite the fact that there were others in the Vatican and in the Church elsewhere who were less so.

On one occasion, when the burden of young people coming to Taizé and the problem of how to encourage them to become bearers of reconciliation when they returned home was on his mind, Brother Roger had the opportunity of speaking to the Pope on the subject. The Prior of Taizé was anxious not to send anyone away into a vacuum. He was aware that the request that people returning to their own parishes should not use the name of Taizé too readily was almost a denial of friendship, and he was aware too that many of the young were failing to find what they sought in their own parishes. He was concerned also that even those for whom Taizé did not seem to offer a welcome in which they felt able to participate should be helped to find an alternative place to go. Yet he was equally concerned that Taizé should not be responsible for creating a youth movement. There were churchmen who, finding their own churches devoid of young people while thousands flocked to the Church of Reconciliation, felt disheartened. The name of Taizé used without tact and sensitivity in parishes, far from effecting reconciliation, could wound and create barriers. Brother Roger confided to the Pope the community's feelings with regard to the onus the young people were thrusting upon them and the brothers' desire to abandon the name of Taizé. Contrary to Brother Roger's expectations, Paul VI was adamant that there could be no question of relinquishing the name of Taizé. 'The Pope', recalls Brother Roger, 'was extremely generous. I dare not say what he said to me because it was of a goodness which in my view was not restrained, but which exceeded all limits.' According to one of the brothers, Paul VI had drawn a parallel between Taizé and Assisi. It was a comparison which others have drawn since, but one about which the brothers themselves are cautious. 'Many members of the community are captivated by St Francis,' one brother confided, 'and there is perhaps something of a parallel in the free, spontaneous way of living. We share with St Francis the fear of schematizing and creating barriers. St Francis also lived at a time when the Church was troubled and he brought about reforms without separating himself from it. Beyond that there is a risk involved in the comparison.'

Paul VI's eagerness to understand the problems confronting young people was a source of great joy to Brother Roger. Hearing of their commitment from the Prior of Taizé, the Pope expressed a sense of his own inadequacy. It is with embarrassment that Brother Roger recalls Paul VI appealing to him at the end of one audience: 'If you have the key to understanding young people, give it to me.' 'He felt,' states Brother Roger, 'unworthy of young people and he wanted so much to do something with them. As for me, I would like that key but I know I do not have it.'

Paul VI loved to give presents. While the Second Vatican Council was in progress, word of the hospitality offered by the Taizé brothers to the other bishops reached the ears of the Pope. A messenger from the Vatican duly appeared at their flat one evening bearing a box of apples and pears sent by Paul VI for the brothers and their guests. One of the most beautiful gifts he gave to Brother Roger was a chalice for the church at Taizé. This the community has kept together with John XXIII's breviary, which was given to Brother Roger by John XXIII's secretary upon the Pope's death. Among Brother Roger's memories of Paul VI, a man who was so 'incomparable a listener' are audiences during which Brother Roger was put so much at his ease that he frequently found himself with his elbows propped on the Pope's desk in what he describes wryly as 'the posture of a peasant'. There is too the recollection of a meeting he had with Montini some time before he was elected to the papacy. At the conclusion of an exchange

117

during which they had spoken of matters which weighed upon them both, among them places where there were no longer any priests, Montini had pointed to a crucifix. 'You see,' he said, 'if things are going badly it is because we men who hold high responsibility in the Church, crucify him so often.' It was a comment which Brother Roger carries engraved upon his heart, together with an adaptation of Paul VI's words uttered at the conclusion of the Council: 'Man is made sacred by the wounded innocence of his childhood.' The word 'wounded' is not a precise quotation from the Pope's original pronouncement but it is one which has found a special resonance in Brother Roger.

When news of Paul VI's death reached Taizé it was evening on the 6 August 1978. In the summer warmth the brothers were eating their meal beneath the trees outside their house. At a whispered word, they knelt with one accord to pray.

After attending the late pope's funeral in St Peter's Basilica, Brother Roger returned to Taizé to be met by a television interviewer who wished to know what he hoped for in the man about to be elected the next pope. 'I would like to be present in heaven,' reads the text of his recorded reply which seems almost to forecast that the new pope would bear the name of John Paul, 'at the meeting of Pope John XXIII and Pope Paul VI. Those two men complemented each other so well that together they would provide something of the picture of the pope we are looking for. At Taizé we would like the pope to be so much the father of all, so universal, that he does not allow himself to be imprisoned by strong resistance either from the old divisions of Christians throughout the world, or from the new ones. Our hope is that he will try to be so much the father of all that we can easily recognize in him a reflection of the face of God. By his life may he awaken to

God the greatest possible number of people on earth.' Brother Roger's expressed hope was that Paul VI's successor would allow a mystical calling to live within himself, that he would be a man committed to the development of humankind, yet a man conscious that he was ensuring the continuity of Christ through a long Church tradition. In that way he would be a father to both the old and the new generations.

The crisis, which in the 1970s induced numerous priests and religious to abandon the Church at the same time as the young flocked to Taizé in such considerable numbers, caused Brother Roger to reflect deeply upon the implications of receiving a large number of brothers or creating a community for women. 'It helped me greatly to understand that we are asked to build with next to nothing. We must not keep those young people for ourselves. We must grow indeed, with the addition of a few brothers each year, because a family cannot live without growing, but we must agree to send other young people into the ordained ministry or to other congregations.' To retain them or even to establish an order of women would have created 'a kind of frustration' amongst certain religious in existing larger communities. For the community at Taizé, Brother Roger insisted, all that mattered was that it should be a very small sign. The desertion of the Church weighed heavily upon him as did the tensions within it; there could be no question of aggravating the issue.

'God', maintains Brother Roger, 'takes care of our cares.' For the Taizé brothers the task of coping with the sheer volume of visitors to the hill, and indeed of fulfilling their role in fraternities amongst the poor and the suffering, was greatly alleviated by the assistance of a number of other religious communities. From the earliest days of Sister Madeleine's letter there were links with the

Little Sisters of Jesus. 'Wherever we lived when we were away we wanted to be near them, to live a life of contemplation like them at the very heart of human distress, amongst the most destitute.' It was the Little Sisters of Jesus, for example, who in 1977 were to find the brothers a vacated shack in which to live on Hong Kong's congested water front. As far as the welcome at Taizé was concerned, for a while help was provided by a number of different congregations who would send two or three of their members to assist for a period, but there was a slight lack of a sense of continuity in the welcome. Then a community, the origins of which date back some 753 years, came to Taizé from Tournai in Belgium. They were committed to the spirituality of St Ignatius Loyola, and their undertaking to serve the Church wherever they were most needed gave them the freedom and scope to embark upon a more long-term relationship with the community on the hill.

For over twenty years the Sisters of St Andrew have had their fraternity in a nearby village and have helped the brothers to welcome the visitors who come from all over the world. 'Without them,' admits Brother Roger, 'we would have been limited in the extreme.' The fact that they are always there, able to make decisions with regard to the welcome, the fact that they know how to listen, to place themselves at people's disposal day after day cannot be valued too highly. They also help with the bi-monthly 'Letter from Taizé' and look after the young women who come and remain at Taizé for one, two or possibly three years and who, like a number of young men, seek for a while to share the life of the brothers or the sisters, helping to provide a welcome for the other young people and possibly considering a commitment to secular or religious service which may well lead them into communities elsewhere. 'In this way,' concludes Brother Roger, 'we have not wounded other communities by creating in them a sort of fear that this afflux of young people would deprive them of vocations.'

It would be impossible accurately to calculate the precise number of people who visit Taizé each year. The records of those who stay the night, for example, do not include those who come simply for a day. It is estimated, however, that a full week in the summer brings approximately 3,000 visitors. The number of participants grows with every passing year, and even the chill of winter no longer seems to daunt the crowds. It is not without humour that Brother Roger calls to mind a German Protestant church leader who some years ago, on seeing the facilities available to visitors, offered to provide the money to create 'more hygienic conditions'. The offer was, of course, declined as all gifts are declined by the community, but slowly, with the passage of time, it has been possible to improve facilities. Currently it is possible to lodge in dormitories, rooms and barrack-style huts some 1,200 people, and at times when the number exceeds that figure there are always tents. No other place in Europe provides a constant setting for the gathering of young people from so many nations, including an increasing number from the East.

The village of Taizé still consists of a narrow winding street edged by a dozen houses built of rough honey-coloured stone, two of which, set on the southern slope of the hill, serve as retreat houses for those who wish to spend their stay in silence. The brothers' home is connected to the twelfth-century church by a passage way which they themselves constructed. They are sufficiently removed from the centre of activity for the contemplative character of the community to be preserved, but on land adjoining the village there now stands not only the Church of Reconciliation and a bell tower, but also a guest house named El Abiodh after the village in the Sahara where once Charles de Foucauld lived, the 'Yellow House' where meetings with brothers take place and where information and a ready welcome is made available, a 'Salle d'Exposition' where the community's pottery, artwork, books and records are exhibited and sold, and a small café that forms a general meeting place. On the meadow land where thousands of sleeping places can be improvised there are also toilets and showers. 'With the years,' smiles Brother Roger, 'the welcome has become more hygienic.'

6

TO THE ENDS OF
THE EARTH

'We love this place, this house, a family house,' states Brother Roger, 'and in our daily effort there is an awareness of tapping a source that is not in us – which God deposits in us but which does not come from us. That source feeds love ... A life of communion with God, a contemplative life presupposes for many, though not for all, the idea of cloistered solitude, isolation from the human family. For us that is not true at all.'

In the village of Taizé there has always been a form of extended family around the brothers. It was characteristic of the community that when the Abbé Buisson – a priest from the nearby village of Culle-les-Roches and the man who in some small sense replaced John XXIII as a spiritual father to Taizé – became old and was no longer fit enough to live alone, the brothers took him in and looked after him as one of their own. When, after an accident, Brother

Roger's mother had difficulty in walking, she too came to Taizé to live with his sister Geneviève. It was an idea which Brother Roger resisted for some time: 'My brothers and I had made the same choice. Why should my mother be permitted to come and not theirs?' Eventually, however, he was induced to concede that he had no right to prevent his sister from looking after a mother who needed her. His mother in her latter years was to continue to leave a profound impression upon him and upon the life of the community, for she was a woman who manifested profound goodness and love towards everyone, and one whose faith – about which she was so reticent to speak – nevertheless communicated itself to all around her by 'a kind of osmosis'.

Brother Roger recalls how on the subject of faith, his mother would often express a conviction which she also passed on to him: 'If in Europe faith is disappearing, it is from Africa that the gospel will return to us in all its freshness.' It was for this reason that she used to like to talk with the young Africans who came to Taizé and make them welcome in the few rooms fitted out for her in Geneviève's house. Her maternal heart was also attentive to each one of the extensive family of boys whom Geneviève had adopted and who were by this time grown up. She had a special affection for the young wife of one of the boys who had herself had a very difficult childhood. After a car accident the young woman had to be taken, unconscious, to hospital. When she came round it was to discover that her few-months-old baby had been killed in the incident, yet her first thought was to ask her husband not to tell her 'grandmother' that the child was dead; the news would cause her too much suffering. Brother Roger's mother was not her real grandmother but the young woman had received so much warmth from her that after a few years she had come to love her like a mother and wanted to spare her pain in her old age.

In October 1973 Brother Roger was absent from Taizé, and while he was away his mother, who had been suffering for some time with a heart complaint, felt her death approaching. In the corner of her small room she saw a vision of Christ. 'I am ready,' she responded, 'but my son is not present. I would like him to have returned.' Her request appears to have been granted, for she did not die until 4 December when she passed away peacefully and without fear while her son was at evening prayer in the Church of Reconciliation. It was the second time that she had experienced such a vision. The first occasion had been when Roger was six or seven. His mother, herself weakened by tuberculosis, had been nursing her own mother who was dying of cancer, and had reached the end of her resources. One night, when she thought she was nearing her end, she saw the figure of Christ who spoke to her saying: 'Do not be afraid, only believe.' She was left with a sense of great peace and very gradually began to recover her strength. With maturity Brother Roger came to realize that his mother's apparent calmness and capacity to surmount adversity concealed private turmoil. The fact that she admitted to him on one occasion that although she might seem serene, she carried within her an inner combat, remains with him still. Perhaps the most pervasive memory left by Amélie Schutz to her son, however, is that of her sheer love of life. Several years before her death, shortly after her first heart attack, she exclaimed, 'I am not afraid of death, but I love life.' 'I too love life,' confesses Brother Roger, 'although not perhaps in the same way as my mother.' It is a source of evident joy to him that some of her qualities have communicated themselves to him, and that many have remarked upon the fact that he is the very image of his mother. Amélie Schutz is buried in the tiny graveyard of the Romanesque church in the village at Taizé where the graves of two deceased brothers are also sited. On her simple tombstone are inscribed the words: 'The risen Christ comes to light a festival in the innermost part of man.'

Beside the older generation, flourishes the new. The brothers themselves now cover a wide range of ages and it is a source of admiration and wonder to Brother Roger that there has never been a gulf between the generations. Dismissing his own extraordinary capacity to communicate in his advancing years with the young of so many nations, he marvels that the older members among his brothers are so adaptable. Next to Brother Roger's room at Taizé is what is known as the 'children's room', equipped with toys and picture books to keep his youngest visitors amused, and guarded by a resident dog. There have always been children at Taizé from the very earliest days when Geneviève first became a mother to the orphans of the war. 'Their story', insists Brother Roger, 'would constitute a book in itself.' For the youngest and the most vulnerable members of the human family he has a special affection, and for this reason the words of Paul VI concerning the innocence of childhood have struck a very particular chord of recognition. For Brother Roger the wounded innocence of childhood finds one of its most haunting expressions in the memory of an encounter with a child squatting in a narrow alley-way in Bangladesh. The boy was holding a baby in one arm and trying with the other to pick up a second infant. With both in his arms, he himself collapsed. Why, asks Brother Roger, is it not possible to care for such children? 'It is true that if I were to follow the inclinations of my own heart I would look after the very youngest children – to try and be with them to soothe them even more than to cure, to transfigure in them the injury of their childhood. It is not necessarily their parents who wound their innocence. Often it is by what they have heard and what they have seen elsewhere that they are hurt. Their ears and their hearts are wounded. God can transfigure and use their wounds, but if I could care for little children it would be to try and avoid such injury.' It is, suggests Brother Roger, the kind of ideal which remains for the most part unrealizable. The community did, however, take in one very sick baby in what he refers to as a unique episode in its history.

In 1976 Brother Roger and a number of other brothers spent a period of time in the slums of Calcutta together with a group of young people from four continents. Brother Roger had felt that in order to embark upon a new stage of development it was essential to write, together with the young people, a letter to the people of God, compiled not at Taizé but whilst living amongst those who knew the most extreme poverty. In this way, it seemed to him that the 'Second Letter to the People of God' would gain a completely different value from that of the first, published at Taizé two years previously on the opening of the Council of Youth. The brothers stayed in a hovel in the slum where Mother Teresa had first begun her work. They also worked amongst the poorest of the poor together with Mother Teresa's Missionaries of Charity. With evident warmth, Brother Roger recalls Mother Teresa making all the necessary arrangements. It was she who arranged for them to receive the reserved sacrament and provided the wooden tabernacle in which it could be kept in their slum house. In the mornings she would join them for prayer. After that, the day would include work in the home for the dying or amongst the lepers for whom the Missionaries of Charity care. Each morning Brother Roger would go with one of the brothers who is a doctor to the home for abandoned and sick children. It was, he sighs in broken sentences, a very poignant experience: 'The children who died in my arms. You do the absolute maximum you can for hours on end and then . . . The cries of those children – their little mouths open just fractionally, but you don't hear anything. No sound comes out, just the faintest of breaths. The death of a child is very hard!'

It was one of these suffering, parentless children that Brother Roger took into his care. 'From the very first day in the home for abandoned children, each day I looked after a very sick baby, a little girl of four months whose mother had died in childbirth. As I held her in my arms I was told that she would surely die because she would never have the strength to resist the diseases of India.' Brother Roger's voice was the first male voice the tiny baby had heard and, despite her weak condition, she responded to it. Seeing this, it was one of the Missionaries of Charity who urged him to take the child with him back to Europe where there was a slight chance that she would survive. As yet the baby had no Christian name. Spontaneously Brother Roger suggested that she should be christened Marie Louise after the grandmother who had meant so much to him. With great difficulty, because of rigorous regulations laid down by the Indian Government, he obtained the necessary permission to bring her back to France. 'The story of her recovery was a very long one. She came very, very close to death. I took her to a specialist in Paris and we did everything we could but she could not digest anything. She vomited everything we gave her to eat. Then she could not sleep. She would only sleep in my arms and when I sang to her she responded to my voice.' For months the little Indian girl lived in Brother Roger's room, slept on his lap as he worked and retained an extraordinary sensitivity to his voice; and gradually she recovered. Marie Louise Sonaly now lives with Geneviève, but she visits her godfather every day. Each noon, of her own volition, she accompanies him to the Church of Reconciliation to nestle beside him throughout the common prayer. Recently, as a result of a virus contracted in the slums of Haiti, Brother Roger was compelled to undergo an operation to remove a cataract from his eye. The experience left him weak and tired in a way which Marie Sonaly sensed profoundly. The first words she uttered that her godfather was able to understand were an entreaty that he should not leave her. His illness brought renewed reluctance to let go of his hand even for the briefest moment. The rupture of human affections in general is something which touches Brother Roger deeply. Listening to the experiences of those stricken by broken relationships causes him a pain which he finds difficult to conceal, and the thought of creating a vacuum in the life of another concerns him intensely. 'If ever I ask God that I may live,' he confides, 'it is for her sake. She is so attached to me and still too young for such a rupture.'

Mother Teresa had been one of the visitors to Taizé some time before the compilation of the letter from Calcutta. The brothers' stay there was part of a continuing and valued relationship with her, a bond based on a common compassion and commitment. Together Brother Roger and Mother Teresa have written prayers and letters giving voice to their shared concern for the suffering and the poverty, both material and spiritual, the 'areas of desert', in the 'Third World' and in the affluent West. Together they have identified the hidden poverty of those societies that lack the spontaneous joy which wells up unaccountably but freely from the poorest of the poor. Together too they have given voice to their shared vision of reconciliation in that unique communion called the Church.

We are both of us challenged [they have written], by the suffering of the modern world. Confronted with all that wounds humanity, we find the division between Christians unbearable. Are we ready to set aside our separations, freeing ourselves from our fear of one another? When people differ, what use is there in trying to find who was right and who was wrong?

In our search for reconciliation, are we ready to learn ways of offering the best of ourselves, of welcoming what is best in others, loving each other in the way Jesus loves us?

The appeal goes on to give thanks for the respective gifts of the Catholic Church as 'the Church of the Eucharist', the Protestant Churches as 'the Churches of the Word' and the Orthodox Churches who 'are brought by faithfulness to go to the very extremes of loving'. More recently in Rome, in April 1984, Mother Teresa and Brother Roger together led meditations on the way of the cross for a gathering of young people to mark the international jubilee. Their united effort is all the more remarkable and eloquent for the fact that Mother Teresa speaks no French and Brother Roger's English is very limited. By his own admission he is not a natural linguist but in a one-to-one situation, face to face with a particular individual, he finds that his timidity recedes. 'I understand a tiny bit of what Mother Teresa says and when we are alone I understand her better.' When all else fails there are always translators available, for many of the brothers are gifted linguists. 'Some of them', explains Brother Roger almost with awe, 'speak five, six, even seven languages fluently. Here we have cassettes and records to help them. I think we like human competence and so we make use of all modern technology. It is part of being passionate seekers after God.' With Mother Teresa, however, there seems to exist an understanding that defies all differences of language and even of vocabulary. 'In many respects they are different,' comments one of the brothers, 'but there is between them an indefinable something that operates at the level of the heart.'

It appears that in Calcutta Mother Teresa tried to extract from Brother Roger a promise that he would wear his white habit all the time. Normally the brothers do not wear their robes when working, but in Calcutta at least, in response to Mother Teresa's view that contemporary man needs visible signs and references, Brother Roger did agree to wear his habit everywhere. In return Mother Teresa herself undertook to make him a lightweight robe. She took his measurements and stitched at least part of it herself. In Europe Brother Roger finds it less easy to wear a habit in the street and in more recent years its white colour has become in some way an embarrassment to him. There are times, therefore, when he has taken to wearing a brown shawl in order to appear 'less equivocal'.

Distinction of any kind rests uneasily upon Brother Roger. In 1974 the news reached him that he had been awarded the Templeton Foundation Prize for Progress in Religion. 'Brother Roger', read the citation, 'has been instrumental in widening and deepening man's knowledge and love of God through his worldwide work among young people and his efforts for renewal and reconciliation and thereby furthering the quest for the quality of life that mirrors the Divine.' Brother Roger himself knew little about the prize apart from the fact that Mother Teresa had been the previous year's recipient of it. Perhaps this fact, combined with the discovery that one of the judges for the prize was the Revd Dr Eugene Carson Blake, former General Secretary of the World Council of Churches and a trusted friend, contributed to preventing him from declining this award as he declined France's attempt to honour him with the *Legion d'honneur*. As it was, the sum of money which went with the prize was not accepted for the Taizé community, nor was it accepted for the reception of the tens of thousands of young people, despite the fact that at the time the welcome fund was empty. Instead, Brother Roger consulted the young visitors to the hill as to how it should be used and at their suggestion it was donated to 'poor young people, especially in the southern hemisphere, who, committed in the ways of struggle and contemplation, are seeking to meet one another and to be tireless seekers of communion'. Part of the money was left in the British Isles, for young people working among immigrants from Africa and Asia, especially Pakistan and also for those struggling for reconciliation in Northern Ireland.

Inevitably, with the passage of time, Taizé has drawn the interest of the press but it is an interest about which the brothers are cautious. The occasional presence of film cameras in the Church of Reconciliation is something with which they have come to terms primarily because it is a means of communicating with large numbers of people who could not otherwise join in the common prayer. Taizé has also, over the years, attracted some extraordinary offers. Numerous inheritances and properties have been put forward and declined as all gifts are declined. One offer, however, touched the community more than most. Taizé was visited more than once by Jacques Hébertot, the founder of the celebrated Hébertot Theatre in Paris and a man whom Brother Roger identified as 'a man of prayer, a man who believed'. Hébertot had had the inspiration of constructing a temporary theatre at Taizé for the summer, in which he could arrange the performance of plays selected by the community. 'The offer was of a generosity beyond words because we would not only have had the choice of the subject matter but of the author too and in the winter the same plays would be performed in his theatre in Paris.' Brother Roger admits to having been moved as much by the goodness of Hébertot's heart as by the actual offer, but for him there could be no question of such an expression on the hill. It was not that he had anything against the idea of a Christian theatre. He was all for the implementation of Hébertot's idea, but not at Taizé where he felt that the attention of those who came to the hill should not be dispersed in directions that were too diverse.

'All I want', exclaims Brother Roger, 'is to be like anyone else.' After receiving the Templeton Prize, he hesitated a good deal before succceeding Albert Schweitzer, Romano Guardini and Paul Tillich as a recipient of the German Publishers' and Booksellers' Peace Prize. He never gives autographs, protesting that he is not a film star or a sports champion; nor does he ever sign copies of his books, and he is always embarrassed when photographed. He does not feel that it is right for churchmen to add to the service of God and their pastoral commitment honorific titles. Ministry in the Church has been too frequently associated with temporal power when essentially it is communion. Above all, he does not wish to be in any way set apart from his brothers. Within the community he does not want to be referred to as the prior and, even outside, the word is used only in order speedily to denote a function. The most recent modification to the Rule substitutes 'servant of communion' for 'prior' and, in keeping with this evolution, Brother Roger no longer wears the cross he used to wear on his white habit as a mark of his office as prior. Members of the community are all, it is implied, with their different abilities, servants of communion and he is but one of them whose particular service is to animate and reanimate with each new day the communion of the whole. Furthermore, when he gives a blessing it is, he insists, as one layman may bless another; and before each journey upon which he embarks it is he who kneels to receive the blessing of his brothers.

Until the age of sixty Brother Roger travelled relatively little. It was only in 1975 that he was led to embark on more frequent journeys and ones which took him further afield. He had always thought that Christians would be reconciled by broadening their horizons, by going out to those who differed from themselves, by being open to non-believers, by carrying the preoccupations of those who were in difficulty and by being attentive to the poorest of the poor. It was the vision of the reconciliation of the whole of humanity which made the effort of striving for reconciliation between Christians worth while. As an end in itself the latter would never have held the same interest. After the opening of the Council of Youth he realized that completely new signs must be found to express the fact that there is only one human family, that the Church is called upon to carry the pain of all men and that one of the essential callings of every Christian is to be a ferment of reconciliation, confidence and peace from one end of the world to the other. In order to express this intuition not merely in words he wanted to give of his person. So it was that he set off to live for periods of time in areas of poverty, in places that were particularly significant, beginning in 1975 with a stay in Chile, a land then stricken by a murderous *coup d'état*, and then in 1976 with a period in Calcutta.

By travelling and meeting people in very different countries he is made constantly aware of the needs, the sorrows and the joys of his fellow men. There is in him recognition of the need to go out to others and so to leave the self behind. Fortunately travel is something upon which on the whole he readily embarks. Flying in particular is an experience which he enjoys. The thought of it calls to mind intermediate landings made during a visit to Hungary and the rest he was able to catch up on stretched out between the tables in a waiting-room. It would, he adds almost wistfully, be nice to cross Hungary in a car. Most of the time, to his regret, he has to leave a country without having really seen anything of it. Yet even the most fleeting of encounters can be turned into a moment of communion. Train journeys conjure up memories of the brothers sharing their food provisions with other travellers – the spirit of festival in dimly-lit railway carriages.

In 1977 Brother Roger went together with a number of other brothers and an intercontinental team of young people to share the living conditions of the poverty-stricken people living in junks on the South China Sea. In Hong Kong harbour they lived aboard an old house-boat and a hut mounted on stilts in cluttered, dirty water. Amongst the jumbled collection of straw mattresses, paraffin lamps and bowls that formed their bare necessities of living, the sacrament was reserved in a 'corner of rare beauty'. The following year Brother Roger went to Africa, where he visited the black districts of Soweto and Crossroads before spending four weeks amongst the flimsy tin-and-cardboard shacks of Mathare Valley, the poorest slum in Nairobi, and discovering amongst the harshest conditions, the hospitality of the poor. So warm was this hospitality that, on his departure, Brother Roger left several of his brothers in Mathare Valley where they lived for seven years in a hut built of old planks, and became fully integrated into a community where they were the only white residents. This fraternity is still in Nairobi but has moved to another place of extreme poverty. Brother Roger's own visit to Africa was concluded with Christmas night celebrated with the occupants of a home for the dying run by Mother Teresa's Missionaries of Charity in Addis Ababa. To those prepared to see, on the faces of the young the crisis in Ethiopia was already visible.

The fruits of the stay in Africa were the 'Acts of the Council of Youth', to which Brother Roger himself added a letter from Africa subtitled 'The Wonder of a Love', for each year, from a place that is a powerful symbol of poverty and distress, he writes a letter to the young, suggesting concrete possibilities for commitment and providing a few basic reference points to which people may return continually throughout their lives. The 'Acts' themselves stemmed from a premise that 'the closer we come to the sources of the Christian life in the contemplation of Christ, the more we are led to look for acts to put into practice in the concrete situations in which we live.' They provided some suggestions as to how the parish might become 'the family of families, the community of communities, where encounter between the generations is possible and the particular gifts of each age-group can be brought to light.' This theme was to become a frequent one at Taizé during the years that followed. Thenceforth young people would increasingly be encouraged to go back to their own parishes and there become the ferment of communion rather than creating little groups apart. The 'Acts' also suggested the celebration of a weekly Easter as part of the endeavour to find 'meditative and accessible ways of praying'. From young people in the countries of Eastern Europe came the idea of prayer around the cross each Friday evening at the same time in each country, as a way of keeping company with the risen Christ who suffers for those in tribulation throughout the world; and, from a visit to the Russian Orthodox churches in Moscow in July 1978, Brother Roger brought back a gesture to accompany that prayer. Thus the text exhorts:

Friday evening pray alone or with others around the cross in communion particularly with persecuted Christians and prisoners of conscience throughout the world. On the wood of the cross, laid flat on the floor, you can place your forehead as a sign that you commit all that weighs you down to Christ, who is in agony with mankind until the end of time.

Saturday evening, anticipate the resurrection by a festival of the light of Christ, with the reading of the gospel of the resurrection and a prayer of vigil, which may last until the following morning.

On Sunday, celebrate in a spirit of festival the risen Lord recognized in Scripture and in the breaking of bread, the Eucharist.

This mode of prayer was subsequently to unite young and old at Taizé and in parishes throughout Europe and beyond. 'The Acts of the Council of Youth' were made public in December 1978 at the first European meeting. 15,000 participants from all over Europe were welcomed into houses in over a hundred parishes in the city of Paris and its suburbs. Thus welcomed into parishes which had been well prepared, young people could have an immediate experience of what the text from Africa proposed to them.

Preparations within the parishes had been going on for some eight months prior to the main celebration which was held in the packed Cathedral of Notre Dame and transmitted simultaneously to another church close by. So significant was this vast gathering for prayer that other similar European meetings were subsequently held: in 1979 in Barcelona, in both the beautiful church of Santa Maria del Mar and a medieval shipyard turned into an improvised place of worship; in 1980 and 1982 in Rome; and in 1981 in London, where prayers were held in St Paul's, Westminster Cathedral and Westminster Abbey. 1983 took the crowds once more to Paris, and in 1984 the chain of these European meetings was continued in

Cologne. The large number of those who attended these gatherings spoke for the enthusiasm of the young people concerned. As for the brothers, they too found the magnitude of the attendance important. Small groups, it was pointed out, can lose their sense of universality. 'Such crowds are a source of encouragement. The encounter might be less deep than an experience at Taizé but there is a reality about being amongst people in that way.' The brothers had also perceived a maturation on the part of those attending the gatherings. An ever decreasing minority were there to see the sights of the capitals of Europe; more and more were present to pray with great commitment. In Cologne, what was said and experienced was taken up by individuals and by the media and discussed far beyond the boundaries of the gathering itself. Thus the encounter was one that was really lived with a wide range of people. In 1984 Christians in India expressed the need for a gathering of young people from all over the world in Madras. Such a meeting would represent an adventure in confidence, conceded Brother Roger, for nothing of the kind had ever before been undertaken so far afield, yet for that very reason, because it was a challenge to faith, a pilgrimage of trust, the invitation could not be declined. Recognizing, however, that only a limited number of young people from other continents would be able to travel to India, a meeting was also planned to be held simultaneously, initially at Taizé. Such was the feeling amongst young people that a European meeting in a great city where visitors were actually welcomed into parishes and local homes, was irreplaceable, that the proposed meeting at Taizé was subsequently moved to Barcelona. The dates towards the end of 1985 were staggered so that Brother Roger could be present both in India and Spain. The rhythm of the annual European meetings continues and the preparations for them, the prayer, the discussion and the searching span the intervening months.

For Brother Roger 1979 had brought with it yet another experience of solidarity and communion in potentially the most distressing circumstances. This took the form of a stay in a poor district of the city of Temuco in Chile, once more undertaken with an international group of young people. It was following this stay that it became apparent that the project for the Council of Youth had been provisionally replaced by a 'pilgrimage of reconciliation', a reality that was more open and accessible to all generations. It was then, too, that Brother Roger wrote 'The Itinerary of a Pilgrim'. By 1980 a pilgrimage of world-wide dimensions was already in progress, but that year was to mark this fact in an even more concrete way. In 1980 Brother Roger joined large congregations in prayer in Spain, Belgium, New York, Washington, Montreal, Ottawa, Toronto, and both West and East Germany. The pattern for successive years was set. So it is that, regularly in the cathedrals of Europe and other continents, hundreds of thousands of people gather for vast prayer celebrations. The pilgrimage is one which assumes ever more universal dimensions, yet it is one which is lived increasingly within the hearts of those who embark upon it. At the end of 1980, from a ramshackle caravan in southern Italy among the destitute victims of an earthquake that wrought terrible destruction in November of that year, Brother Roger wrote a 'Letter from Italy' in which he urged people to set out as 'pilgrims of reconciliation' – not necessarily far from their own homes but there where God had placed them.

'Dresden', recalls one of the brothers, 'was a particularly moving experience for us.' The Lutheran Bishop of Dresden, who is currently one of the presidents of the World Council of Churches, has been a special friend to

Brother Roger. One of the brothers was able to travel to East Germany for the first time in 1962, at a time when access was not easy. He visited a number of people there, and, identifying in them a sense of isolation, he suggested to Brother Roger on his return that frequent visits should be made, if only on a more or less private basis. Other brothers were to follow and relationships were gradually built up both there and in other Eastern bloc countries. In East Germany the Bishop of Dresden wanted Brother Roger to come and speak more publicly. However, authorization was not obtained until 1980, when Brother Roger was able to speak to 6,000 young people in the large church in Dresden in a celebration that went on late into the night, and to other equally sizeable gatherings in Leipzig and in the Catholic and Protestant churches of Erfurt. So moved was the Bishop of Dresden by the experience that afterwards he was unable to speak. Together he and Brother Roger put on a record and sat listening wordlessly to music. Since then the visits to East Germany have become something of a tradition and Brother Roger returns there every year.

On the occasion of Brother Roger's seventieth birthday one of the Lutheran bishops in East Germany wrote to him as follows:

> I thank God for all that I have received from you along my own spiritual path. The prayer for reconciliation in the cathedral of my city, with so many young people, their intense silence and their singing, are among the most profound impressions of my life. In particular I remember what you said to them of the pastorate in which all may participate. I have also retained the memory of your comment that each person, even though he may have understood very little of the gospel, has received gifts sufficient to render another attentive to Jesus.

It was a letter which together with that of another Lutheran bishop from the same country was to enhance the happiness of Brother Roger's birthday although no doubt both said 'nice things' of the kind which Brother Roger insists he must try to forget at once:

> Together with so many young Christians we give thanks to the risen Christ for having enabled you to be for many young people in numerous countries the upholder of a life penetrated with contemplative silence. And on this your birthday none of your brothers can be separated from you. I know that the poor, the maltreated and the suffering in particular will not forget you and neither will the children, nor, in our country, the young people who are so dearly loved.

'Bari', Brother Roger casts his mind back, 'was another very beautiful page in our life.' At a time when the brothers were insisting that they did not wish to create a movement around Taizé, that they wanted the young people to give priority to their own parishes, it was almost inevitable that the community should feel itself impelled to try for itself what it was asking of others. 'We were living the common life, we were a monastic community. We could not transport ourselves into the parishes and yet how could we say what we were saying without going at least once into one of them?' A brother was sent to explore the possibilities of a very poor district in a parish in Bari in southern Italy. The parish had a church but no resident priest and the congregation consisted of some elderly women, a few younger women and one man. A potential home for the brothers was found in a nearby house that had stood unoccupied for twenty years. The ground floor was solid enough but only parts of the upper floor were sound and the flat roof was unsafe to walk upon. When the twenty brothers arrived, however, they set about cleaning it up and with the help of the local people created a place in which they could live 'an exceptional experience'. 'Those who received us in the parish did wonders. They brought mattresses and cardboard which we put under the mattresses and cellophane to replace the broken windows, but there were no toilets, water, nothing. Everything had to be improvised.' Before deciding upon Bari, the brothers had ensured that they would be able to work for their living. And so in the mornings they swept the southern Italian streets as part of a team of local road sweepers. 'They didn't receive any less money because of us but we helped them, were a kind of presence among them, with the result that within a few days friendship was born.' The church gradually filled. The brothers held their thrice daily prayers there and sometimes in the evening it was packed to overflowing. After prayers a meal was provided, of necessity very improvised because of the limited cooking facilities. It was eaten, not in the house because there was insufficient room, but outside in the street there was a little for everyone. 'We might have a saucepan of spaghetti,' remembers Brother Roger. 'Then afterwards there were apples, but never enough. We had to cut them into two, sometimes into four, but we shared the little we had.' There are memories too of the local women who liked to go and pray the rosary in the church. The brothers would join them, thus associating themselves with the prayer 'which already existed', and afterwards the Taizé prayer would be celebrated. After the departure of the brothers the daily prayer continued and goes on to this day in the poor districts of Bari, uniting each day at the same time the ancient traditional prayer with a more modern form. Furthermore, from that prayer gestures of solidarity have sprung, acts of sharing with the poorest of the poor and visits to other parishes. 'Those weeks left a profound impression. It gave us the confidence to continue with that slightly strange intuition of sending young people back to the parishes.'

Other places conjure up equally vivid impressions and what Brother Roger refers to as 'little flashes'. Haiti, for example, where Brother Roger lived amongst people who were not merely poor but utterly destitute, calls to mind once more the old women 'who do not feel that they have accomplished anything in their lives'. Their hidden fidelity, their hearts that are like treasure and the fact that they are often considered of such little value evokes in Brother Roger the desire to thank them for being so valuable in the life of the Church. 'The woman who is advancing in years has such an important role to play.' 'Why do I feel like this?' he sets himself the question. 'Perhaps because I discern in them the fact that they have known how to love, how to traverse trials, and I sense in them something of the plenitude of God, of which they are often unaware. Their life is full of a serene beauty.'

The United States has been a land of Brother Roger's dreams ever since as a small boy his grandmother told him of his great grandfather's voyages to Boston. In imagination he has walked the cotton fields of the deep South. In reality his experience of the States has been of life in Hell's Kitchen, New York: strident cries in the night and serene prayer in St Patrick's Cathedral.

Of Belfast, where he went before the European meeting in London, and Dublin, which he visited for a gathering of young people in May 1985, he says: 'Over the years at Taizé we have come to know a number of Irish people, and unlimited confidence has been born. God has deposited in each individual a unique gift; in the same way he grants gifts to each nation. We admire the zest for living in so many young Irish people who are yet so scarred by economic recession and harsh unemployment. To the Irish people God has granted the gift of rising above discouragement.'

London recaptures images of welcome: the bells of St Martin-in-the-Fields rung so vigorously in recognition of the brothers' presence that the room in which they were staying immediately next to the church shook with the vibrations. Prior to the stay in London, however, came the first European meeting in Rome, a city whose welcome must represent a highlight in the history of the community. In many respects this meeting was similar to those held previously in Paris and Barcelona. Approximately 30,000 participants flocked to Italy to stay with families and communities in and around Rome, to share in the life of the parishes and to pray together. Prayers were held twice a day simultaneously in the basilicas of St John Lateran, St Mary Major and St Mary of the Angels. Brother Roger spoke in each of them in turn, and his address in each case was relayed immediately to the others. In Rome special emphasis was given to the link with the early Christians, and on 29 December a day was spent in a spirit of prayer and recollection in the city's catacombs. The pilgrimage represented a direct response to Brother Roger's invitation in his 'Letter from Italy' to seek a 'childhood of the Church', a childhood that was not, however, a nostalgia for the Church of the early ages, but rather a state of openness to heartfelt confidence, simplicity, the wonder of a love, jubilation, the love of life closely linked to the desire for the living God.

On the following day St Peter's Basilica was packed with people of many denominations, and outside in the cold of St Peter's Square there waited several thousand more. Pope John Paul II was to join the young people gathered there in prayer. The European meeting in Rome was a means of offering young people a more concrete role

144

in helping to foster reconciliation between Christians. Furthermore, it was for the brothers a significant demonstration of confidence in them on the part of the Vatican. 'It is also interesting,' one of the brothers points out, 'that several years before the first European meeting Brother Roger had said in the course of an address: "We are awaiting the day, we are hoping for the day and we are sure that the day will come when the Vatican can be a place of welcome as vast as the world."' Some time later, at a meeting in Paris, Brother Roger had expressed his regret that there was not a church available that was large enough to accommodate all the young people who would like to attend the European meetings, and the man who had himself captured the hearts of so many young people was quick to invite him to Rome. 'The welcome we were given during that European meeting, the fact that so many parts of the Vatican were placed at our disposal and that the invitation was repeated,' continues the brother, 'gave new meaning to a sentence which at the time seemed perhaps a little too poetic.'

As Bishop and Cardinal of Cracow, Karol Wojtyla had twice visited Taizé prior to his election as Pope, and Brother Roger, for his part, had twice been the guest of the Cardinal in Cracow. On the hill of Piekary not far from Cracow an annual pilgrimage is held. The participants are Upper Silesian miners who journey to a Marian sanctuary while the women wait and pray in the surrounding parish churches. 'The bishop there', recounts one of the brothers, 'is a very courageous man. He invariably invites someone from the West to be present at the pilgrimage and the Cardinal of Cracow always attends.' On the first two occasions when Brother Roger participated in the pilgrimage, the Cardinal in question was Wojtyla. Brother Roger's first visit, during which he led a meditation on the Virgin, also involved a three-day stay in the bishop's palace in Cracow. The second visit, though shorter, was no less powerful. Before the assembled masses on the Polish hillside Cardinal Wojtyla spoke out in strong and urgent terms and Brother Roger was called upon to speak immediately after him.

Brother Roger had already identified in the Cardinal of Cracow the gifts of the man who was not so very long afterwards to become Pope John Paul II. The election of the Polish cardinal brought with it the reflection that John Paul II was so passionately interested in his contemporaries and so pastoral. He would be able to bring a breath of universality to the Church.

On the eve of his enthronement the new Pope was host to a number of delegations among whom were Brother Roger, Brother Max and several other brothers. 'Praised be Jesus Christ for giving us so good a pope,' Brother Roger greeted John Paul II. 'Brother Roger,' came the response, 'come and see me often.' Brother Roger was on his way to Africa at the time and so they spoke for a while on the subject of Africa, and then the Pope gave a short talk for everyone present. At the end of the address he appealed to the whole assembly, 'Before parting we are all going to hold hands as a sign that we want reconciliation.' Turning to Brother Roger in search of confirmation John Paul II added, 'Don't you agree, Brother Roger? Let us be reconciled.' It goes without saying that Brother Roger's answer was unqualified agreement.

Since then Brother Roger has been a guest of John Paul II on numerous occasions. The Pope has, insists Brother Roger, 'a great capacity to grasp, to understand the mentality of today'. In his encyclical *Redemptor Hominis*, John Paul II has gone so far as to affirm that Christ is united to every individual without exception, even if that person is not conscious of the fact. By so doing he has dispelled the long-standing source of contention which implied that God was reserved for an élite. In terms of extreme clarity he has shown that through the coming of Christ the love of God became a source of salvation for all men of every nation and every race. To Brother Roger such a statement is a long-sought-after source of hope for a Church that exists for the entire human family.

At the end of the month in which news of the attempt on the Pope's life shocked the world, Brother Roger was once again due to go to Poland to take part in the miners' pilgrimage. Having heard that the Pope would almost certainly recover from his wounds, he asked whether it would be possible to visit John Paul II in the clinic in Rome. The reply came back that he would be welcome to do so on his return from Poland. Brother Roger arrived late for his appointment because his plane had been delayed, but he came bearing wild flowers gathered in the Pope's homeland. 'I discovered that the Pope was hurt much more gravely than I had supposed. Had I known his condition I would never have dared to ask to see him.' As it was, the encounter was to prove to be one of the 'most beautiful moments' of Brother Roger's life. It brought with it the revelation of a profound love and great confidence. 'Perhaps', adds Brother Roger, 'because I am a few years older than the Pope and therefore closer to the end, closer to eternal life.'

Recently there have been regular audiences between the two men. 'The subjects of the texts presented to the Pope vary,' one of the young brothers who has accompanied Brother Roger to Rome on a number of occasions elaborates, 'But they raise questions such as: How can young people be helped to discover all that the Church can be, a theme which is a great passion of Brother Roger's. How can the Church be a ferment of communion not only for those who believe? How can new roads to reconciliation be found? How is it possible to live reconciliation within oneself? The format of the texts,' the brother continues with a smile, 'is likely to be more in the nature of a child's letter, for Brother Roger would have difficulty in compiling documents that are very official. The value of the meetings lies in the fact that it is essential that the Pope should know directly what is happening, that he should not hear distortions. By this means Brother Roger can tell him what preoccupies us very simply, without resorting to long texts. There are, after all, certain things that the Pope can do that others cannot. He can surmount certain difficulties that no one else can.' Inevitably the statement prompts the question as to whether the Pope has in fact surmounted those difficulties. 'Brother Roger says that when John Paul II reflects aloud he goes very far, which is a sign that we can have hope.'

7

THE WONDER OF THE COMMON LIFE

Like the readiness of young people to make arduous journeys to kneel for long hours in the draughty cathedrals of
distant lands, the continued presence of the visitors to the
hill of Taizé remains a source of amazement to the community of brothers who now number approximately
eighty in all. 'We go to the church late at night and find
them praying in the half-darkness. They are there long
before the common prayer begins and long after it has
finished, and there are just as many to listen to in the cold
of winter as in the summer months. Why do they come? In
search of God, the spirit of the living God, that unique
essential that is sometimes so hidden from our eyes. They
come to question themselves a little and sometimes to
unburden themselves.' The brothers do not give the
sacrament of reconciliation, but each night Brother Roger
and a number of other members of the community remain

in the Church of Reconciliation long after the evening prayers to listen to anyone who wishes to speak to them. To Brother Roger the experience is a treasured part of the discovery of God through others: 'I do not want to live without being with people, without accompanying them, without listening, without being captivated within. Sometimes when I am listening to people I do not know what the time is. I do not want to know.' The most wonderful part of the gospel message is that God loves us unconditionally; the worst experience in life is that of being abandoned, and so listening becomes not a psychological dialogue or a question of analysis but the shared search for the mere beginnings of an answer and the realization of the love of God. 'Something in someone else's heart, that has perhaps been blocked, is coming to the surface. The discovery that nothing can separate him from the love of God. That is the essential thing. All else has little importance. How can he come to understand that in him the essential is accomplished?' The response once again takes the form, not of solutions easily or authoritatively offered, but of that still small voice in which God speaks. 'To listen to others is not to force, to oblige them, but to accompany them.'

If he had taken notes of all that he had heard in this way, Brother Roger admits, the material would have made many interesting books. Listening to the young, the brothers have frequently been made aware of events germinating in the world at large. The troubles of 1968, for example, were foreshadowed by the preoccupations of those who brought their concern to the Church of Reconciliation. Nothing, however, is noted down and rarely is any question raised beneath the icon in the church discussed by the brothers. 'Why this silence?' asks Brother Roger. 'So that people know that what they disclose is said in the presence of God.'

Each evening, at the end of a day that officially begins at 8 a.m. with morning prayer, the brothers invite a number of male guests to join them for a simple supper. Female guests are entertained on a similar basis by the sisters. In recent summers, however, because of the numbers wishing to talk in the Church of Reconciliation, the meal timed for 10 p.m. has often been delayed until shortly before eleven. Sometimes, too, there have been as many as fifty or sixty guests with the brothers. The increase in numbers has taxed the energy of the community to the extreme and there is very little time for even the minimum amount of rest. 'Where do you find the energy when too many demands are made upon the body?' sighs Brother Roger. 'I believe you draw it from shared trust, confidence, the confidence of the young people who have come here over the years which is renewed each year.' No one really understands why there have been so few problems with the visitors who come to Taizé. At night a number of young people are available to ensure that all is quiet, but that is all that has been necessary.

There is energy to be drawn too from the common life, from the trust that exists between the brothers and from contemplative expectation. 'A frequent question from young people,' recounts Brother Roger, 'relates to the fact that they have no confidence in themselves. It is a very delicate one to answer. To myself I say, "Do they know that it comes from somewhere apart from themselves, that it comes from the spirit of the living God, the presence of the risen Christ who accompanies us. We can submit all our worries to God, find rest in him." In theory the Christian should not worry, but then,' he smiles, 'man is full of contradictions ... Today', he adds, 'I have confidence. God always gives. It is only we who do not always perceive the priorities, and when the weight of work reaches the very limit of human strength what remains of enduring importance is that inner silence, the peace of Christ and compassion should not be lost, for without them all else would vanish.'

For Brother Roger the path of struggle and contemplation is easier when lived with others. Alone it is more difficult to do much for others. Together in the common life, quickened by the love of Christ, a way forward emerges that leads from barrenness to shared creation. Reaching out to others means leaving the self behind. What is repeatedly stressed, however, is that such a process does not mean self-destruction. The brothers may all be very different, but what the community seeks to achieve is a means of making of those differences not obstacles but stimulants to creativity. The personality must not be repressed. One man must not be a destroyer of others, rather each must be constantly attentive to the others so that members of the community do not create in parallel. The impression may be that the brothers are thereby limited in the realization of their individual gifts, but the underlying insight is that man never fulfils himself without resistance and that in the community that resistance comes to him through creation in common. The human personality must not be destroyed; nor must it be given a completely free reign to fulfil itself, for that would not be communion but separate development under the same roof.

The range of the community's national origins is remarkable: out of eighty brothers there are representatives of some twenty nations and several come from distant continents. Their range of abilities is no less impressive. There are several doctors and engineers, musicians, artists, brothers with expertise in fields ranging from agriculture to ceramics and writing, from computer science to sociology and theology. A small computer operates at Taizé to assist with, among other tasks, the preparation of the text for the 'Letter from Taizé' in its nine different languages, and its subsequent distribution to 130 countries. The community runs its own publishing house and a ceramics workshop as part of the effort to be financially self-sufficient. To this effort Brother Roger himself contributes his writings and, as part of his share of the practical functioning of the community, it is still he who chooses the colour of the paints and arranges the interiors of the buildings in which the brothers live.

It was to allow scope for the development of many skills and to enable brothers of many denominations, nationalities and cultural backgrounds to live together, and at the same time to ensure that the whole was not merely a juxtaposing of individuals but really a parable of communion, that the *Rule* was written in its original form. More recently Brother Roger, in his search to retain only what is essential, has altered even its title, since he sees it not so much as a Rule in the usual sense but rather as a simple way of living a parable of communion. It is now known, therefore, as the *Sources of Taizé*. The absence of formalized rules characterizes the brothers' entire life together. No stipulations are made as to the kind of person who may enter the community. Often a young man considering entry will live for several months among the young people on the hill, but there are no regulations regarding his conduct. It is a question, rather, of an intuitive understanding of all that living together implies.

Entry into the community involves a simple ceremony at evening prayer during which the new brother is clothed in his white liturgical vestment and becomes what is known as a 'young brother'. Again, there is no formal novitiate period. It is recognized that individuals mature at different rates and that some are ready sooner than others for permanent commitment. It is a matter for the individual brother and for the community to decide when he is ready to be professed. In the mean time he lives a life that is almost indistinguishable from that of the remainder of the community. There is no hierarchy between the old and young and no reluctance to give even the youngest considerable responsibility. Older brothers are, however, specifically designated to accompany young brothers and to prepare them for the day when they are ready to make formally a series of promises that have changed little since the first brothers committed themselves for life to Christ in the community in 1949:

Will you, for love of Christ, consecrate yourself to him with all your being?
—I will.

Will you henceforth fulfil your service of God within our community, in communion with your brothers?
—I will.

Will you, renouncing all ownership, live with your brothers not only in community of material goods, but also in community of spiritual goods, striving for openness of heart?
—I will.

Will you, in order to be more available to serve with your brothers, and in order to give yourself in undivided love to Christ, remain in celibacy?
—I will.

Will you, so that we may be of one heart and one mind and so that the unity of our common service may be fully achieved, adopt the orientations of the community expressed by the servant of communion, bearing in mind that he is only a poor servant in the community?
—I will.

Will you, always discerning Christ in your brothers, watch over them in good days and bad, in suffering and in joy?
—I will.

Such restrictions as these promises do impose are seen not as something negative but rather as a means to plenitude. It is recognized, for example, that now perhaps more than ever, celibacy cannot be looked upon primarily as a question of self-mastery but as part of the great mystery of Christ and the irrational of the gospel, and in the all-embracing light of the transfiguration. There has never been any mention of obedience in the Rule of Taizé. Instead, the community asks for the brothers' acceptance that the pastoral task of continually recreating the communion of the whole be entrusted to one man, a 'servant of communion'. One of the services of that man is to help each brother to discover his gift so that he can use it freely within the common creativity. 'We do not think so much of Brother Roger as being at the head of the community,' explains one of the brothers, 'as being at the centre of it. We are inspired by his vision and he is very good at expressing what the community is trying to live. He is a man who listens and he has an extremely practical side to him, but if he has gifts that others have not, the reverse is also true.' Brother Roger is searching with his brothers. Together they are seeking to mature in the common life and in their 'adventure with God', and so no brother is looked upon as more advanced than any other.

Frequently, when Brother Roger speaks in public, a number of the brothers provide a simultaneous translation in several different languages. It is characteristic of him that he should have suggested to his interpreters that they should feel free to change anything he says if they felt that they could express it better. His brothers are naturally reluctant to do so, but there have been times, it is intimated with a smile, when Brother Roger has returned to a subject already well covered and those interpreting have not felt inclined to follow suit. Such is the relationship between Brother Roger and his brothers at a very practical level.

To those who visit Taizé, part of the attraction of the community undoubtedly lies in its ecumenical nature. However, of all the reasons volunteered by visitors as an explanation for their presence, that most frequently heard is the strength of the prayer. Its intensity is something which strikes even the brothers when they return after periods of absence. They have remarked too upon the fact that over the years the common prayer has of its own accord grown considerably longer, as if borne along by the commitment of the many visitors. With the help of a musician in Paris and inspired by the awareness that not everyone who comes to Taizé understands French, the community began a search some years ago for a service in which people of all races and denominations could join. Out of that search evolved the present liturgy with readings of biblical passages which are of necessity short – because they are frequently repeated in a number of languages – and are selected with 'a pastoral heart' which appreciates that there are certain biblical texts that are not readily comprehensible to those not well-versed in theology. A long litany drawn from traditional liturgy is sung each day. Each request is expressed in another language and concludes with a *Kyrie eleison*. Music and the singing of meditative chants begins before the bells chime the call to prayer and continues after the service has officially ended, a fact which reinforces the impression of the great continuity of a prayer that has no beginning and no end. The simple musical themes and Latin phrases or short sentences in various European languages are easily learnt, readily repeated and have a tendency to remain with the singer long after audible sound has ceased. Thus they meet the requirements to be both popular and contemplative. Also they have no specified end and are brought to a conclusion only by the interposing of an 'Amen.' Without any conscious effort to achieve that effect, many different elements have combined to produce the impression of a mantra, perhaps because, as one of the brothers put it, 'the prayer of repetition is more universally rooted in mankind than we might think'. Brother Roger speaks of his own discovery that, for many, a prayer repeated ceaselessly can be an invaluable means of sustaining an inner life. For some it is the uninterrupted Jesus prayer. For others it is 'Hail Mary, full of grace'. For yet others it takes the form of a prayer sung collectively which leads spontaneously into the silence of the heart.

Silence has a vital role to play in the prayers at Taizé. Its ready use is based on the recognition that human prayer is inevitably poor and that explicit prayer is reduced to very small dimensions by comparison with the immensity of the secret prayer of Christ in every person. Essential prayer may thus take place in a great silence in which Christ is enabled to pray in the individual with the confidence of a little child. In this way also the anguish of a sense of inability to pray is dispelled, for in the silence of the heart Christ whispers, 'Be not afraid for I am here.'

Every possible attempt has been made to prevent the thrice daily prayer from appearing mechanical or rigid, qualities which experience has shown to be unacceptable to today's generations. Brother Roger recounts the anecdote of how, as part of the endeavour to avoid the mechanical, instead of doing it himself he invited one of the young brothers to give the signal to conclude the several minutes of silence kept in the middle of the thrice daily prayer. Deep in contemplation the brother remained kneeling long after the silence would generally have been brought to an end. Brother Roger admits to waiting anxiously in the knowledge that his other brothers were tired and in need of rest. 'That', he smiles, 'is the common life.'

Beyond the noise and the bustle of the crowds, the strumming of innumerable guitars and the sound of laughter and chatter resounding late into the evening, there is at Taizé a central core of peace. In part perhaps that peace is due to the quality of the Burgundy countryside but much, it may be suggested, is attributable to the tranquillity that emanates from the community itself and from that 'inner silence' which Brother Roger has said is 'the realization of the mystical life, the life of communion with God, about which so little can be said'.

Intimations of a childlike awe enter his voice whenever he speaks of his brothers – of the brother, for example, who looks upon what others might regard as a succession of painful trials as 'a progression from discovery to discovery.' 'Only a mystic speaks like that,' marvels Brother Roger. There is wonder at the quality of those whose life he shares and at the fact that it has been given to him to share it. 'They are', he reflects, 'all beings whose life is given and I am deeply moved to see in them throughout the day a reflection of the sanctity of the Church, of Christ in them. I am confounded by the fact that it has been given to us to live with men of such transparency.' Among his happiest memories he counts walking in open fields or through the streets of some vast city, gathering at the end of a day to talk in the kitchen of the brothers' house, and the look of transparent honesty on a brother's face as he enters a room.

Their life together calls for great spiritual tact and delicacy of touch. For each it involves of necessity struggle and contemplation and therefore inner combat. At times they are called upon to traverse such inner trials alone.

There are times in consequence when Brother Roger asks himself whether they are not in fact too reserved towards one another. That is not, he insists, what the brothers want. They seek a way of transparency. They do try, however, to avoid letting their own burdens weigh too heavily upon others. 'In the common life', he adds, 'one cannot carry everything together with explicit words but each should be able silently to discern in others, to understand the fight because it is there for each one of us. Sometimes it happens that a long time after an event, it becomes possible to talk about it. That is cause for great happiness because everything is realized at once – one has not wanted to hide anything. Yet if one has kept silent it was in order to breathe, and to allow others to breathe, to allow others not to lose the joy of God, to advance along the path. Those moments when we have to keep silence are moments of an unbelievable inner solitude. Surrounded as we are, loved, supported, borne along, there is still no escaping moments of inner solitude. Silence is necessary. How can we hear God without that silence? When I was young I wrote down the words: "Love solitude, detest isolation." There are times when we ask God to take these worries, to take that which is preoccupying us, and he takes them but still they dwell in us and at that moment we discover inner solitude, isolation, and at that moment we need to be led to God by another, to be accompanied in another way without necessarily having to disclose the details of what is causing us pain, by someone who senses what we are going through.'

There are in the common life moments of great joy, moments which Brother Roger describes as 'essential'. The common life expands the heart. 'For my part,' he confides, 'I can be suddenly joyous for no reason. It does not take anything in particular. I am happy to be alive, happy about what we are, happy to see the beauty of those faces, to admire everything that they are and to know them all so well. It is like an inner song. Not every day, but at times it is like an inner song – and that communicates itself.'

At any given time a substantial number of the brothers are away from Taizé living in fraternities scattered across the continents. In 1985 there were brothers living in New York, in Alagoinhas (Brazil), in Nairobi and also in Asia. There are brothers living in Calcutta, not far from the place where Brother Roger himself stayed for a while. Others are in Dacca, the capital of a Bangladesh that is constantly afflicted by famine, drought and floods. The most recently formed fraternities are in Seoul and Tokyo, places which once again involved a new stage in the community's development because, being so far away, they presupposed an acceptance by the brothers concerned of less frequent returns to Taizé.

On the whole, such fraternities are only initiated following an invitation from a country for the brothers to live a contemplative life among the poor there. Often the fraternity includes young people who share that life. In Europe there are brothers in Rome, who since the European meeting have been invited to share in the pastorate of the young people in the diocese. In Geneva, Brother Max works in the theological department of the World Council of Churches. He has been closely involved in the preparation of an ecumenical text on 'Baptism, Eucharist and Ministry'. In Eastern Europe it is not possible to establish an actual fraternity, but brothers travel to and from there throughout the year. 'The brothers in fraternity', explains one of the brothers, 'try to share their life with people who feel themselves abandoned, to accompany them. It stems back to the very earliest days when Brother Roger took in refugees. The young people who come here are often wounded and in need of companionship, but the wounds encountered in the fraternities, which are often placed in some of the most stricken sectors of large cities, are more visible.'

The same brother had suggested that there was something of the poet in many members of the community, and the attractions to those poetically inclined of a place where everyone is called upon to use his imagination to arrange the little he has to bring gaiety into life are self-evident. Yet Brother Roger repeatedly stresses that the community must not become a place where life is too easy or comfortable. Perhaps then the fraternities must be viewed in this light also. 'If a proportion of our brothers did not share the life of the poorest in this world,' the brother continues, 'we would not be able to live what we live at Taizé.'

Because of their experiences and encounters with the suffering of this world, the brothers are extremely sensitive to injustice. They have not hesitated to speak out on the subject nor even to give concrete expression to their concern by working with trade unions and others involved in social struggles. As in the Gospel parable of the leaven, their role is to penetrate society in its entirety and there proclaim in communion the joy of the risen Christ.

Once a year all the brothers who are able, and at least one from each fraternity, return to Taizé to spend a week in council. The council never broaches questions of administration or organization. Rather it is an interval during which the brothers seek together to express the essential sources of their common vocation. 'In between,' smiles the brother, 'we do a lot of letter writing.' News from the fraternities is shared over meals, and experiences gleaned elsewhere are used to enrich the life of the community at home.

After their experience of sleeping in an improvised dormitory on the South China Sea, many of the brothers slept for several years in dormitories at Taizé. Indeed some of the young brothers from Asia had never slept in any other way. For members of the community it was a way of being together and held for them associations with those who were called upon to watch and remain awake with Christ. An icon, illuminated throughout the night, served as a symbolic reminder of this intention. As the day started with the first words uttered at morning prayer, so it ended with prayer together. Recently, however, the dormitories have been abandoned; Brother Roger had noticed that certain brothers were not sleeping well and lacked adequate rest. Sleeping in the same room as his brothers was an experience which he himself shared for a while and valued, but it was better for him to cease doing so because he sleeps so little. Night-time for him is often a time of walks beneath the stars and contemplation in solitude.

From the very beginning of Taizé, Brother Roger accepted that nothing could be accomplished without a process of maturation and that the community must progress one day at a time in the knowledge that it was only little by little that Christ would become their essential love. They must, he knew, be prepared to love Christ without seeing him and so grow in Spirit. The history of the brothers' life together is characterized by a continual search for the mode of existence which might best make that growth possible. Certain elements within it are constantly changing and evolving. There was, for instance, a time in the early days of the community when the brothers assembled to pray in the middle of the night. It was a practice which they saw as a means of expressing 'the gratuity of prayer', but one which they were subsequently advised to drop for very practical reasons. The rhythm and requirements of their life now would make regular prayer in the night too demanding, but the practice is relived at certain times of the year and it is continued in a sense by the young people who frequently take it upon themselves to pray through the night. Often, too, some of the brothers will remain in the Church of Reconciliation into the early hours in company with those who have chosen to pass the night in contemplation. Other practices, at first considered necessary as signs to help maintain the religious life of a new community, have also been relinquished, partly perhaps as a result of an awareness that a change in the psychological structure and the religious consciousness of human beings has taken place over the centuries and that it is not, therefore, necessary to be over-impressed by the religious practices of bygone ages. Partly, too, such changes have been due to a quest for simplicity, not simplicity for its own sake but a simplicity that is inseparable from joy and from mercy, and which might enable the community better to live the spirit of the Beatitudes. The Vatican Council itself evoked much discussion of the 'Church of the poor', yet even then it was fully recognized both that poverty in itself was not something positive and that the Church could not be looked upon as exclusively for the materially poor. The Church must be a Church for everyone and above all it must seek simplicity. The compilation of the 'Letter to the People of God', deliberately undertaken in Calcutta, a city where many are poor in the extreme yet possess joy, generosity of heart and spiritual wealth, was to bring with it an encounter with 'witnesses to another future' and the attempt to introduce into the life of the community something of the 'song' that issued from the lives of the poorest of the poor.

The search continues as does the creativity. In their different ways, more recent years have been as creative as the first, and perhaps the brothers are still learning how better to integrate their individual creativity into the whole. The need even to mention the names, individual skills and varying backgrounds of particular brothers is no longer felt. Yet to Brother Roger such progress is but a step along the way and by no means the conclusion of the journey. 'What is true is that every moment of my life, from the very instant I rise, I marvel at the way God has led us to this common life, and sometimes I ask myself, "Have we begun it?" Now,' exclaims Brother Roger, 'I would say "yes". We are in the very preliminary stages. We are still in the infancy of our progress towards that parable of communion and our attempt to achieve it without wounding anyone. Sometimes,' he adds with undisguised regret, 'we wound without intending to.'

In the light of his advancing years, Brother Roger had already, some time ago, given considerable thought to the leadership of the community after him. After consulting numerous brothers he has committed a suggestion to paper. The name of the person concerned will remain undisclosed, however, until after Brother Roger's death. 'I have no fears for the future of the community,' he insists. 'My brothers all have what is needed.' Then, almost as an afterthought, he adds, 'Now, perhaps for the first time, I sense that all my brothers love me. Not in a particular way but I know that all my brothers love me.'

On the floor of the Church of Reconciliation, the brothers kneel in double file at the centre of a growing congregation. Watching Brother Roger enter and greet with the lightest of touches those whom he is encountering for the first time of the day, it is difficult to doubt the reciprocity of that love. In the silent union of so many, the 'parable of community' becomes recognizable and understandable without verbal explanation.

There were some questions perhaps more aptly posed of Brother Roger's brothers. Did they, for example, share in his positive vision of the future of the community after his death? The capacity of the community to deal with whatever trials might arise appeared to be something in which the brothers had great confidence. Although Brother Roger's vision is unique, there is every reason for the community to be certain of its continuation. Brother Roger himself has done much to encourage his brothers to deepen their own intuition and, in his unfaltering wish to be no different from his brothers, it was intimated, he had to a very large extent succeeded.

The nature of, and difficulties associated with, authority seemed to be one of the issues which had concerned Brother Roger and the community deeply. At a personal level, it was disclosed, Brother Roger is acutely conscious of the difficulty of remaining himself in the presence of large gatherings of people of prominence, although less so now than in his younger days. The disclosure called to mind Brother Roger's own assertion that the real self was not the façade reflected each morning in the mirror but rather the deeper 'me' whom God loves and calls by a name. 'God has called each one of us by a name at birth. We may not know that deep me, but God calls forth the response from that me – grant that I may give myself.'

Taizé has always been careful to avoid all visible links with the power of money or politics. Yet Brother Roger recognizes that there is a distinction, for example, between belonging to a particular political party and making a stand for human justice. No attempt is made to deny the reality of political power and, when it is a question of defending a victim of injustice or preserving peace between nations, Brother Roger does not hesitate to intervene with those who hold it – be it with Mrs Gandhi, with General Franco, with the President of El Salvador, or with representatives of the two 'super powers'. 'Following the beginning of the worldwide pilgrimage of reconciliation in 1980 there were meetings all over Europe,' a brother recounted. In the course of these the question arose as to whether it would be appropriate to make an appeal for reconciliation and peace not only to churchmen but also to political leaders. At the meeting in London the issue was highlighted by the fact that it coincided with the arms talks in Geneva between representatives of the United States and the Soviet Union. It was decided, therefore, that Brother Roger should try to see representatives of both countries. What was of paramount importance was that he should not meet representatives of one world leader without seeing those of the other. For this reason it took several years before a meeting with ambassadors from both nations was finally achieved. In April 1983 in Madrid, Brother Roger, accompanied by Marie Sonaly and a number of other children representing the different continents of the world took the following appeal to the ambassadors of the Soviet Union and the United States of America to be transmitted to Mr Andropov and Mr Reagan respectively:

Our ardent aspiration is to find a way out of a spiral of fear and to open up paths of trust.

For the sake of children throughout the world who cannot speak for themselves about the threats to their future, I have come here with some children to present this appeal to your ambassador in Madrid. I have come to appeal to you to do everything in your power so that the innocence of childhood will not be wounded, and so that nobody in the world will ever be a victim of the incredible power of the destructive forces of war, some of which can annihilate a portion of humanity.

The possibility of using advanced scientific techniques to attack human life has caused a violent crisis of confidence: peoples come to be afraid of one another, and heads of state experience the same fear. In the end, human beings even become afraid of their own fear. The result is a withdrawal into oneself that is occurring everywhere; creative capacities are frozen by fright.

And yet the whole human family wants peace, and never war. Those who want war are only a few. There are multitudes of people, young and old, who know that world peace is engendered by confident trust between all the peoples of the earth, and that this peace depends as well upon a fair distribution of the goods of the earth between poor regions and rich regions. And there are multitudes of people who would like to open up paths of trust and also take part in this fair sharing.

But it is true that some wonder whether placing their trust in political leaders does not make it easier for them to abuse this trust with respect to peoples. In order to find a way out of the spiral of fear and to open up paths of trust, there is thus an immense need for the certainty that political leaders will have unlimited love and compassion for the entire human family, with no exceptions.

Today, for a world population which is growing in numbers day by day, a continual development of science and technology is so important. Science and technology can either destroy or build up: it all depends upon the use to which they are put. They can contribute to such great good, for example by discovering methods of intense agricultural production adapted to local situations, or, among many other possibilities, by finding ways to alleviate or to cure physical or moral suffering . . . Science and technology can even serve to broaden a passionate interest in the human being and in the universe as a whole which can help turn back the tide of fanaticism.

In the face of the fear that freezes so much creative energy, it is urgent to open paths of confidence between all human beings, and urgent to share justly the goods of the earth, in order to make the earth a place fit to live in for all.

With this end in view, I venture to insist that, together with children, the elderly man that I am may be able to come and meet with you yourself. It is so essential, with no delay, to do all in our power to prepare a future of peace and to open up, with children themselves, brand-new ways of reconciliation.

'At that time,' said one of the brothers, 'a meeting of young people was being held in Madrid as part of the worldwide pilgrimage. Brother Roger was staying in a poor apartment and his neighbours were a young couple who had a tiny, premature baby. At the very last minute Brother Roger decided on impulse to take the child with him. While the meetings were in progress, the baby's mother waited anxiously outside. The two ambassadors themselves, however, were very touched by the sight of the six children. In fact the Russian ambassador sent for his own grandchildren to come and join them.'

In July 1985 Brother Roger also visited the United Nations to be received by its Secretary-General, Mr Perez de Cuellar, to whom, once again with a group of children, he conveyed an appeal for world disarmament and a number of questions which expressed the expectations of a multitude of young people with regard to the role of those who are in a position to create trust rather than hostility between nations. Well aware of the limitations of such symbolic gestures, they are nonetheless symbols which, in the name of children who have no voice concerning the threats which jeopardize their future, he feels he must seek.

'Brother Roger', volunteered the brother, 'is interested in such subjects as science and technology, in recycling and the latest theories on nutrition.' He recognizes that it is not scientific or technological progress that menaces but rather the use that men may make of it. 'The Christian', Brother Roger has said, 'is not an idealist. At the same time he does not reject hope for humanity. He is interested in humanity because Christ has fashioned him with a universal heart.' Perhaps it is part of that profound interest, part of the fact that he is not a man of illusions, that Brother Roger's diary entries and the written prayers which he now regards as the most appropriate means of personal expression, include references to darkness, inner poverty and shadows. The message is ultimately one of hope; but alone, in the solitude of his room, he can suffer with Indian refugees, with Muslim and Christian brothers fighting in Lebanon and with the victims of violence in Northern Ireland, and who will know of his constrained emotion? The closing of his door at night is a moment that he seems to look upon almost with apprehension. Was solitude in general something that he experienced unreadily? 'To each', responded the brother, 'his night, and Brother Roger has said that belief means consenting to that night. He loves to be with his brothers but at the same time he recognizes that there is a place of emptiness in each of us that no human relationship but only God can fill. Somewhere in that part of our being that is like no other person, Christ awaits us.'

Beyond the ready smile, I had sensed in Brother Roger the marks of the constant challenge to his resources. Was there perhaps the beginnings of a parallel to be drawn between him and John XXIII, the pope to whom he had referred as a prophet rejected, a man of vision whose prophetic ministry had not met with the response for which it called? It was a purely personal impression and one which I knew Brother Roger himself would emphatically refute, not only because the comparison with one whom he held in such high regard would have embarrassed him greatly but also because he does not like the epithet 'prophetic' to be applied to him, insisting that it is only long afterwards that a thing or a person can be pronounced prophetic. I knew too that after the death of John XXIII there had been a suggestion that the bishops had left him on his own; Brother Roger may not talk about those things which touch him deeply straight away but he undoubtedly has the support and the solidarity of the community. If inevitably there are moments when the trials of his existence weigh more heavily, it is also true that, as the very history of Taizé will confirm, he has an exceptional ability continually to renew, to recreate and, in personal terms, to 'bounce back'. He has, after all, the health and temperament of his mother who brought warmth and vitality to all around her into her very old age.

One attribute in particular has struck many who encounter Brother Roger, namely his possession of the 'spontaneity of a childlike heart'. If anything, that childlike heart would seem to have become more manifest, over the years. It is a capacious heart characterized not only by spontaneity but by confidence in God, trust and hope, and which for that reason allows even in moments of trial, perhaps particularly in moments of trial, for unlimited possibilities.

'In your darkness', proclaims Brother Roger in his 'Letter from the Desert', 'a fire is lit which will never be extinguished. You who would be the bearer of a fire into the very nights of humanity, will you allow an inner life to grow within you?' The continual growth of that life, insists Brother Roger, is the supreme human adventure. It is a life that has no beginning and no end.

8

AN AGE THAT COUNTS

Seated beside the fire in the quiet seclusion of his room, Brother Roger told me, 'I like the age I am now. It is an age that counts.' Inspired in part perhaps by his mother's attitude both to this life and to what is to follow, he has no fear of death but rather carries in him the unshakeable conviction that death is sweet repose and the passage into a new life. At this time nothing frightens him: neither death if it is to come soon, nor life if it is still for years to come to lead him to animate the parable of the community and to conceive ways of reconciliation as yet unknown. Furthermore, as the years advance upon him, at last he feels that he has learnt a vital lesson; he has begun to know how to love more disinterestedly. His journal referred to other compensations. 'Why fear the physical degradations,' he had written, 'when age brings with it an inner vision?' The reminder of this earlier reflection evoked in him, as so often, the need to qualify and question. Had his inner vision really grown with age? He dwelt upon his own inquiry: 'I am not very sure. I know only that in those moments in our common life that are very full, I am acutely aware of the Latin words: *Ubi caritas, deus ibi est;* where love is, there is God, there he is visible. There is also an awareness in me that the inner life with God began with the very quest for confidence, trust in him, and with the initial possibility of carrying, creating together.' The inner life to which he referred had, he felt, begun when he was very young and perhaps only been confirmed by the years. As to the form that confirmation took, the subject was one about which he had difficulty speaking: 'To speak about the mystical vision is very delicate because people think at once of "mysticism". Cautiously he implied the distinction between the mystic path to God, the inner way of the gospel as exemplified by St John of the Cross or St Teresa of Avila – who did not, he pointed out, seek to make of the inner vision that was theirs a doctrine, a system applicable to others – and the mysticism which he saw as an egocentric quest, an attempt to go directly to God without the human family, without the Church, without others. 'For some', Brother Roger added, 'the confirmation of the inner vision may sometimes take the form of visions of Christ, the Virgin or of God.' He accepted the authenticity of such visions, but felt they must be kept carefully in perspective, recognizing that it is not necessarily those who see God who are saints; most of us are asked to believe without seeing. As for psychic experiences, they do not interest him at all, for they involve 'playing with the humility of a God who grants us a choice and who always speaks to us with discretion'. Manifestations of the Spirit of God must not be forced. For Brother Roger the essential is and may remain hidden from man's eyes. For him such inner vision as is granted is linked to the intuition that enables us to understand another's pain without many words. It is related too to the search in which, only little by little, it becomes possible to discern the length and depth of a love that passes understanding. The prayer that is at the very heart of the life of the community is primarily an attitude of expectation which allows the 'Come, Lord!' of the Apocalypse to well up in human beings day after day. It is not the privilege of the few but is accessible to all and expresses itself in a great plurality. So it is that day and night gestures made for Christ become prayer: acts of forgiveness, reconciliation, the struggle to remain faithful in celibacy or in marriage – these become a language addressed to Christ, an indication of love and a response to the question which Christ asks of everyone, ever since he first asked of Peter: 'Do you love me?'

'Faith', explained Brother Roger, 'is basically an inner attitude, confidence in God. We know that through an attitude of welcome towards the God, whom St John tells us loves us, and towards others, we can be united with him.' For this reason and because of the individuality of every human being, he intimated, techniques or methods of prayer should not be sought after. 'Certain exterior attitudes might help us to offer ourselves body and soul. At the end of Luke's Gospel, when Christ parted from the disciples, we are told that they prostrated themselves with their foreheads touching the ground. This is an ancient attitude of prayer, the prayer of the body, a symbolic gesture of the gift of self which can help us to say, "Into thy hands I commend my spirit," but we should not make of such attitudes methods to be imposed on or even suggested to others.' In the Church of Reconciliation brothers and visitors alike kneel, sit or prostrate themselves in whichever of these postures they find most conducive to prayer, for prayer must not be allowed to become mere words, nor must it lose its sense of spontaneity or mystery. The avoidance of rigid forms and imposed methods leaves room for the prayer of gesture and posture, intuition and poetry.

Did such a path not involve, however, a degree of spiritual maturity which not everyone possesses? Were there not some who, in their search for that certain silence of the heart within their daily lives, needed something more defined? The response was born of a sense of his own poverty: 'Oh, when we no longer know what to do, yes, there might well be a need for a little pedagogy, but always momentarily and provisionally.' His fear was that those who, albeit for love of God, placed themselves under the direction of spiritual masters ran the risk of 'entering into that process whereby everything is constructed around oneself and others may be forgotten, even God himself may be forgotten because he is no longer necessary'. Certain techniques of breathing might bring with them a certain peace. If they relaxed the body, why not use them? As always, he would be reluctant to dismiss anything through reaction. What he saw as undesirable, however, was the elevation of such exercises to 'a recipe, a school' in the course of which the means become the end and the individual lives for himself. 'The gospel speaks to us in quite another language. It calls upon us to accept from our vantage point of vulnerability the great mystery we are to ourselves; it does not suggest to us steps that ultimately will not lead us to the desire and the need for the living God.' At that point where he can dispense with God, the individual is aligning himself with mysticism. 'I have', professed Brother Roger, 'never seen mysticism lead to God, only to the self. We start from ourselves and our projections want then to create a God in our own image.'

The strain of talking was taking its toll on his voice.

There was fatigue in Brother Roger's eyes yet he remained intensely alert, craning forward on his pine stool in eager expectation. After a life-time of struggle his was enthusiasm in the true meaning of the word, *en theos* – the God within. Looking back on that struggle, was it conceivable that he could have no regrets? 'Regrets, no,' the suggestion was seized upon almost before it was uttered. 'There is no love of our neighbour without the cross, but Christ can make creative use of everything. He transfigures everything. Even if there are human setbacks, God makes use of everything, it is up to us too, to light a fire with the thorns that pierce us.' Was there then a value in human suffering? 'Ah, there is nothing more difficult than answering that question. Can a God of love inflict suffering? No, we know it isn't he who is responsible. But oh the suffering, the inexplicable suffering of humanity, of little children . . .!' He went on to speak of a Freudian psychoanalyst who, during a visit to Taizé, had been asked to speak on the subject of suffering on the basis of his professional and personal experience of it. The conclusion he had offered was that 'all that we suffer is with a view to greater love within the human family'. Tentatively, in recognition that there was little he could say to those unprepared to accept such an insight, Brother Roger outlined a miracle at work in the world. 'What can we reply to those who do not believe? Nothing, because set answers such as "Think how much greater other people's suffering is than your own," do not really help. Perhaps momentarily they touch the rational in us but they do not sustain. You cannot constantly refer to some greater suffering when you yourself are suffering. Such language is moralistic and does not stem from the gospel.' Confronted by human suffering we are often at a loss for words. For Brother Roger, however, it is then that the miraculous can make itself apparent: 'Christ is with us. He accompanies every human being and he has compassion. Compassion means to "suffer with", and often I say to myself that if Christ were only that, only a Christ of compassion, that would be enough for me.' Christ suffers with those in pain and anguish and is present in the compassion we are called upon to offer our fellow men. 'It is given to us to respond to the suffering of others, not with a hardening of the heart, nor with pity – because pity is an alibi, a perversion of compassion – but with that compassion, the capacity wordlessly to carry another, that is a reflection of God in humanity. To harden one's heart is to harden the very depths of one's being, for the heart is everything. It is as vast as an ocean. But to reach out beyond oneself to be close to another, to be a reflection of God for another, is to go far.'

He spoke of how for reasons we frequently cannot identify, an event may provoke in the heart 'a great ground swell which, as in the ocean, surges upwards from the depths to the surface of consciousness'. 'And the more we seek to understand another,' he concluded, 'the more alive the heart becomes, the more alive our consciousness becomes.' 'Had he', he inquired, 'explained himself a little on suffering?' 'Perhaps a very little,' he volunteered with a sigh that brought movement to his entire body. 'It is', he continued after a pause, 'in the nature of the Christian vocation not to turn in on oneself. To follow Christ is to opt for love and to love is to suffer with another, but not with everyone in general, not with the whole of humanity lest we dilute everything to the point where there is nothing left! God entrusts to us a few. We all have someone to accompany. That is the way that God has granted us to realize ourselves, by loving others not with an easy love but with a love as strong as death. The love of God is given by him and it passes through those he entrusts to us. So it is that we are opened, a way opens for us to love God more purely with a mystical love, a mystical vision.'

It was, Brother Roger admitted, a subject on which during that summer of intense demands made upon the community, he had reflected much. He had spoken of accompanying a few, but to how many did he lend a listening ear in a week alone? Without the love and compassion of others could this man, who strove so manifestly for a heart that was universal, have become the companion of popes and little children? Not for the first time the question was pre-empted: 'God also grants to us someone to carry us, someone to accompany us with that look of compassion, that readiness to listen from the heart. I, for my part could not live without that. As a child I was often afraid to overburden my family by showing what I was going through, but that was how it was in those days. Our upbringing required that we did not show what touched or saddened us.' 'And now in the common life?' 'There is something very deep-rooted in me which means that often I feel it would be better to try and extricate myself all alone in the presence of God, but then I am forgetting the Church which accompanies us, I am forgetting communion. There are moments when one must turn to God alone, moments when no other person can help, but those instances must not be allowed to be prolonged. At such times I tell myself "You are embarking on the way of mysticism, not on that of a mystical vision of God and the Church, but the way of mysticism which seeks direct union with God alone."' At various intervals in his life, Brother Roger acknowledged, there had been older people, outside the community, in whom he had been able to confide. 'Now I think that, laden with years as I am, I ought to be able to manage alone, but no, the way is still the same: consent, consent to the fact that God has not placed us here to carry the burden alone. Paul VI, speaking of the Church, said that it was 'ecstatic', in other words it only lives when it issues forth from itself. God makes of us beings prepared to be ecstatic. That is not to say, beings in ecstasy, but beings prepared not to be static, not to be immobile in misfortune but to transcend and go forth from ourselves.'

Gradually, dimly, there emerged the vision of mankind bound together by shared suffering, compassion and companionship in the Church, that body which Brother Roger sees as the only place capable of being the leaven of communion and friendship for the entire human family, the mystical body of a Christ who came to set all men free, not only those who live explicitly by his example but all men of all races and all nations of the world. Was the disparity between such a vision of harmony and reality as he perceived it still as great? As far as reconciliation was concerned had he seen any real progress? 'With the great ecumenical wave that accompanied the beginning of the Vatican Council we hoped for reconciliation between the Churches, but we have had to accept that that way was impracticable.' He had spoken earlier of another way, a way which no longer seemed to lead so much through ecclesiastical institutions, but one which he saw rather as a way of reconciliation within each individual person. 'Where can we find a road to immediate reconciliation, even the smallest way possible, for a time of transition? Such a way exists,' Brother Roger explains in his most recent book, *A Heart that Trusts* (1986),

It is not an easy way out. It does not consist in a watering down of the faith, since it always presupposes the same faith, the same thinking and the same hope. This little way forward can only be a personal one, an inner way. It is the way of reconciliation within oneself, in one's own being. Without humiliating anybody, without becoming a symbol of repudiation for anyone, we can welcome within ourselves the attentiveness to the Word of God, so dearly loved by the Church families born of the Reformation, together with the treasures of spirituality of the Orthodox Churches, and all the charisms of communion of the Catholic Church, in this way disposing ourselves day after day to put our trust in the mystery of the faith.

'Last year', Brother Roger recalled, 'I was invited to an assembly of the World Council of Churches in Canada, and what astonished me was to see there so many faces that were like icons of Christ.' The existence of such 'icons' amongst church leaders meant that the hope of reconciliation between the Churches need not be abandoned. There were, too, significant gestures – the fact, for example, that a Polish pope could preach in a Lutheran church – which Brother Roger saw as indications 'that it is possible to discern that something will happen one day'. 'The Church is undergoing a long process of giving birth. It is seeking very hard now.' Its horizons, it was implied, were beginning to broaden to embrace the expectations of many of its members.

What, however, of the many young people who were turning to the East? 'The Church too is turning to the East, to that millenary tradition of prayer, the great tradition of the churches of the East. I am confident', Brother Roger confided, 'that we are no longer at point zero. The Catholic Church, non-Catholics and non-Christians are beginning to talk to each other and that is the first essential step. Tolerance is the beginning, and perhaps one could look upon prayer as the common starting point, particularly the prayer of repetition.' Brother Roger admitted to being profoundly touched by an experience of Ramakrishna, the

Hindu mystic of the last century. 'Nothing had prepared him for it and yet towards the end of his life there appeared to him a vision of Christ in agony.' Brother Roger's own universal vision of a Christ who came to set all men free includes the understanding that in the life hereafter we may well be surprised to encounter those who, without having known Christ, lived by him unwittingly. In the heart of God, is not the Church as vast as all humanity?

For the time being, however, the way of reconciliation for which John XXIII had striven, is something which Brother Roger no longer anticipates. 'History has marked the mental structures of the whole of Christianity so profoundly that the way for which John XXIII and the Council hoped is not the way that has imposed itself. Today there are such good documents. Theologians have worked hard – there are theologians among my brothers who have laboured diligently – I would like to mention all their names but in particular that of Brother Max, a life-long companion to me. Together we have lived through so many events that sometimes I say to him, "We are like two faithful battle companions".' Theology remains important to Brother Roger. In the common life theological research becomes a possibility for reflection. The community recognizes readily that there are many theologians, including a number of the young brothers at Taizé, who are capable of comprehending modern aspirations and making the language of faith more accessible. As a means to reconciliation, however, it is felt that what is now needed is not so much theological documentation as the readiness to enter into 'that hidden way, the way of forgiveness, that is so much at the heart of the gospel'.

Ever since he was very young, Brother Roger has tried to make a point each day of reading short passages from the writings of St Teresa of Avila and others who have brought him inspiration, passages to which he often returns. That morning he had read an extract from Dostoevsky in which the author describes a child who is dying of tuberculosis. The passage had found a special resonance in Brother Roger: 'When his mother is full of anguish at the approach of her child's death, the child speaks to her and what he says I could read and never tire of re-reading.' He showed me a piece of paper in which he had transcribed some lines from *The Brothers Karamazov*:

> Each one of us is guilty before everyone, for everyone and for everything and I am more so than others . . .
> It is out of joy and not out of grief that I weep . . .
> I can't explain it to you, for I don't know how to love them.
> If I have sinned against everyone, everyone will forgive me . . . therein is paradise.

'Taken to the extreme, out of context,' Brother Roger explained, 'such words might well seem morbid, a kind of exacerbation of the sense of guilt – which can indeed arise in the life of Christians – but placed in the mouth of that child they assume a totally different resonance. That child says to his mother: "Each one of us is guilty before everyone for everyone and everything and I am more so than others." There he has an extraordinary sense of solidarity with the entire human family. Everyone's transgression is his also and he will not condemn those who have made him suffer in his childhood, who have wounded the innocence of his childhood. The words have something of the prophetic about them. Then it is out of joy that he weeps and he goes on to say, "I can't explain it to you." I love that so much,' exclaimed Brother Roger, 'because one can explain so little in the Christian life. In the evenings I see all those young people. I listen to them and I am asked to speak, but I cannot explain anything beyond myself, for their situation is not mine. I might introduce them to paths in which they would go astray. I cannot help you by example. "If I have sinned against everyone, everyone will forgive me," concludes the child, "therein is paradise". The joy of God is that everything is fulfilled in us.'

'"Happy are those who believe without seeing." We belong to a generation when there is doubt – I sense more and more questions – but we are also in a generation which lives those words of Christ to a very large degree. Ours is a period in history which does not have many signs compared with the period of Teresa of Avila, and so those words of Christ touch us to the very depths. Happy are you, the joy of Christ is there for you, you who are in a situation in which you can give him your confidence without seeing. What marks this generation is their desire not to wear masks and their humility. They can understand the words Dostoevsky places in the mouth of a child about to die. They have a sense of solidarity with the entire human family, and that sense is made concrete in acts that are humble, discreet, hidden – something which it is marvellous to discover today.'

Brother Roger spoke of a development at work in the consciousness of humanity which meant that in recent years individuals had become more fully a part of the human family. 'Man is more concerned about what is happening elsewhere. Sometimes that concern is just an alibi to appease his conscience, for there is always a reverse side to the most beautiful medal; but in general people's consciences are much more sensitive to what the human family is living throughout the world. In that way a great and beautiful mutation is at work.' He spoke of the uncertainty that threatened the future of the young, of economic crises and the menace of the misuse of scientific discoveries which can even lead to the creation of unbelievable weapons of war, and of the maturation without which nothing could be accomplished. 'Maturation can be

described in two words. You see it in old people who
know how to suffer, how to share in the suffering of
others. It is plenitude and is serenely beautiful. Furthermore, many of the young of the new generations are
already on the way, and when maturity comes even in
youth, it provides beings who do not toy with other
people, who do not play at being magi, do not seek to be
gurus to others and give them all sorts of advice, but who
are attentive, ready to listen.'

For Brother Roger it is this readiness to listen which is
essential for contemporary humanity, an openness which
is reinforced in the elderly by the fact that approaching
death dispels the need to lead every idea back to the self
and so renders love less self-centred. In this readiness is
contained more than a hope. 'When the aged open their
homes to a single drug-addict to provide a listening welcome; when the elderly welcome a young person who has
experienced the rupture of human affections, who is
wounded to the very fibre of the heart; when the elderly,
rather than become subject to human isolation and abandonment, know how to open their homes and even
timidly, without embarrassing the person they are with,
remain in silence to pray without imposing that prayer –
then all the ways are open for us to go forward.' When
older people know how to advance without spiritual pre-
tensions and the young of an open and honest generation
reach maturity then, claims Brother Roger, 'the way is
open and we will emerge from an impasse in which
Christian institutions have found themselves as if
blocked. . . . So there it is,' he added with evident excite-
ment, 'this immense hope that is a reality.' It was a reality
that began at the level of the individual and rested upon
the readiness of the people of God to make of their homes
'domestic churches', places of prayer and humble
listening from which to venture out on small pilgrimages

of confidence. 'When we listen to the young day after day, when we venture far away from Taizé to prepare celebrations and meetings, we know that there is nothing euphoric about our situation in the West, but it is through this same situation that the way of humble listening has been found.'

Somewhere beyond human apprehension and the need to rationalize lies the essential. 'And what is the essential? It is that, ever hidden from our own eyes, the will of God be accomplished – "Thy will be done on earth as it is in heaven" – that we consent to circumstances, not in such a way that we say that they are of God, for evil, pain, war, violence, hatred, torture do not come from God, but that we accept that even in such situations the will of God can be accomplished. We can build even with the harshest events. Not only the events that make us happy, but also the most unbearable situations – and even failures – can become dynamic elements that urge us on. Creative energies are somehow reawakened by them, leading to a transfiguration of the world.'

If an individual perceives another according to his own heart, Brother Roger's vision of man and his environment betrayed the extraordinary dimensions of his. Amidst all the contemporary human agony he recognized – he still perceived – the good. Man, he insisted, is a creator and so, as surely as his discoveries pollute water and air, he will find the means of rectifying it. 'We are', he said, 'in a period when analysis of mankind appears generally pessimistic. A pessimistic reading of contemporary history or of humanity's tomorrow often captivates in some way. It fascinates because such an interpretation gives authority to those who formulate it.' An optimistic reading on the other hand carries little weight in the face of all the violence, injustice and destruction that threatens the world. 'An optimistic reading is almost impossible. It hopes for unhoped-for possibilities.' It depends perhaps on confidence in that hidden life in man which mysteriously raises his hopes and expectations. Nevertheless, Brother Roger insisted, neither optimism or pessimism were really of the gospel. The gospel way was one of consent with the confidence of a little child. There was, he felt, little for him to say about the future. It could not be controlled and yet he did not fear it, for the simple reason that youth and the future are one. In the years to come would there still be faith on earth? It seemed to him that there was no answer but to persevere with the young who come in their thousands to Taizé. The community had been called upon to sow without concentrating on the harvest. 'I really do not know', he concluded, 'why things have developed in a way that no one foresaw. In the early days I did not envisage so much of what has happened, but I am conscious that my vision is subjective and that is why contemplative expectation is so important.'

From the tower on the hill, at the centre of the curious assortment of buildings, barrack huts and tents, the bells were ringing. Cautiously, lest his invitation appear in any way an imposition, Brother Roger inquired whether I would like to join in the evening prayer. Outside the brothers' house we parted and went our separate ways to the Church of Reconciliation, but for a moment I watched his slightly stooping form striding briskly along a path beneath the trees, his white robe clearly visible in the fading light. Briefly there came to mind an incident which Brother Roger himself had recorded in his journal. At dusk in Bangladesh a Sufi had come to him. 'All men have the same master,' the Sufi announced, 'As yet it is still an unrevealed secret but later they will realize.' This said he vanished into the night.

EPILOGUE

Since the completion of the final chapters of this book, the proposed meetings in Barcelona and Madras have taken place as part of a 'Pilgrimage of Trust on Earth'. 20,000 young adults from all parts of Europe gathered in Barcelona at the end of 1985. A further 10,000 assembled in Madras from 27 December 1985 to 1 January 1986. Of these, approximately 9,000 were Indians from every province in the subcontinent. The remainder included representatives from twenty countries in Asia, from most European nations, and from other continents also.

The Christian community in Madras had been preparing itself for this event for more than a year, and the young guests were received into religious institutions, parishes and families throughout the city. Each morning, from all over the suburbs pilgrims converged upon Loyola College in Madras, a Jesuit college set in a campus of grass and trees. In the absence of a cathedral large enough to accommodate the crowds, a giant *pandal* – a construction of bamboo and interwoven coconut leaves – was erected and splendidly decorated with an icon of the cross and with garlands of flowers, oil lamps and incense sticks. In this improvised cathedral prayers were held twice daily. The Taizé canons and litany alternated with Indian and oriental singing, and no less than twenty-five simultaneous translations were made to convert Brother Roger's meditations into the numerous Indian and other languages of those assembled there. Yet language and race seemed no longer a barrier, but rather a reflection of that unique communion which is the body of Christ, his Church.

The meeting was an indication of the astonishing vitality of the Asian Churches, and an opportunity to gain an insight into a land where Hinduism is the majority religion and the two million Christians represent a mere 3 per cent of the population; a land also which, despite its remarkable technological and economic development, remains a country of extreme poverty. It was also an occasion destined to break down many prejudices: divisions existing between young people from the towns and those from the country, between the various Christian denominations, and between Indians and people from the West.

In between the gatherings for prayer, young people of so many different cultures, traditions and languages had the opportunity to meet and talk, to explore the substance of the letter that would be compiled from Madras, and to discuss such issues as 'How is it possible to break with all forms of fatalism or passivity in the face of divisions of every kind?' In order that they should not in any way burden the poor who welcomed them so warmly, the visitors took back from the meeting each day a portion of boiled rice to share with their hosts, carefully wrapped up in a leaf.

Brother Roger himself had elected to stay in Kutty Street in Nungambakkam, a slum area with open drains, where disease and mosquitoes are rife. He had, after all, come to Madras not on any mission but primarily to share in the life of the poor. There, in a tiny, old, tiled house, preoccupied by all that surrounded him, he conceived two new projects, ideas which would mark a new and vital stage in the history of Taizé and to which, as so often, his own words give most effective expression:

On Christmas Eve, in the tiny house where we were staying in Madras, with a small slum tight up against it, I was very preoccupied with what we were living with our neighbours. It was at that moment that I told myself, 'What risk can we take?' Until that 24th December, I had never dreamt of either of the two projects which follow:

An Intercontinental Council for Sharing

When the human family is plunged into enormous tensions, when miserable poverty goes side by side with immense individual wealth, and when the population growth rate in certain countries is on the increase as it is in India by twenty million each year, then a sharing of material and cultural goods is demanded by conscience. A sharing which humiliates no one, but which supports everything that promotes human dignity, trust and peace on earth. With women, men, young people and children of every continent, we shall be searching for the way which permits us to go the farthest possible in this sharing.

Appeals and fund raising for the sharing of material goods are becoming more and more frequent, but at the same time reservations towards them are emerging.

Many people doubt whether the funds gathered by certain appeals reach authentic development projects which make possible paid employment (where it is needed) and which cover the vital necessities of food, clothing, lodging, education, medical care, etc.

In Asia, a competent man who, in his own country, is in charge of the distribution of funds coming from appeals, said: 'It is often the cleverest ones who already have a house who manage to get a second one through donations.'

Rather than getting discouraged or, worse still, giving ourselves alibis for selfishly holding back our resources, it is important to try to give assurances about the appeals that are sure. They do exist.

To arrive at a vast sharing on all the continents, competent women and men of all ages are needed. So many adults, young people and even children are eager to take part in a huge sharing effort, and without any age segregation. For example, there are people who are retiring and who are often full of energy for a worthwhile cause.

A council is going to be created to stimulate participation from all the continents and to sum up the best of the suggestions. It will be called the Intercontinental Council for Sharing. It will begin working in autumn 1987, following the intercontinental meetings which will take place in Taizé during the summer of 1987. Before that, a secretariat will be set up in each continent: in Asia, in Bombay; in Africa, in Kinshasa; in Europe, if possible in Warsaw; in Latin America, in Caracas; in North America, in New York; in Australasia, in Melbourne; with regional secretariats in other places.

First of all, it is a question of supporting what exists rather than creating a new appeal. The Intercontinental Council for Sharing will accept no donations for itself, no gifts, nothing. Rather, it will direct people who want to give towards the most reliable of what exists. Obviously, secretariats involve travel expenses and a minimum to live on for those who run them. The costs cannot be covered by an appeal for donations. Communities living uniquely off their own work and accepting no gifts for themselves, not even their own family inheritances – in a word, who accept nothing – will meet the material costs.

There remains the enormous question of cultural sharing. Every country in the world has its own particular cultural gifts. To discover ways for this sharing to take place, it would be preferable to rely on a large existing organization, UNESCO, considering that here too it is a question of bringing forth the best of what already exists. This organization is currently going through a crisis but is trying to re-establish a balance. If necessary, other avenues could be explored with a view to the sharing of cultures. In autumn 1987, it will be possible to say which direction to move in with regard to this question.

The Gandhi Prize

Also on Christmas Eve, I was wondering how we could encourage someone or a body of people who dedicate themselves to establishing trust between all peoples, to bringing forth reconciliation and to promoting sharing of goods. The idea came of establishing a prize which will be given every January 1st. The prize bears the name of the Mahatma Gandhi; it is called the Gandhi Prize.

This January 1st, the prize has been given to a Polish lady from Warsaw, Aniela Urbanowicz, born in 1899. Without counting the cost, she gave herself in the Polish resistance during the Second World War. During the

bombing, she saved human lives, while her own husband and daughter were dying in Auschwitz. Even
today, in her old age, she is still giving the best of herself
to sustain a fine human hope among many people.

To you all,
 with heartfelt trust,
  Brother Roger of Taizé.

INDEX

192

194